JESUS BURGERS

true stories of

LOVE, REDEMPTION & MIRACLES IN A COLLEGE TOWN

Sea Hill Press Inc.

Sea Hill Press Inc.
www.seahillpress.com
Santa Barbara, California
Book design and layout by Walter Sharp

Cover photography by Josh Morton
Cover design by Tony Hui

ISBN: 978-1-937720-08-7

Printed in the United States of America

WE HIGHLY RECOMMEND YOU WATCH OUR VIDEO TO GET A GLIMPSE OF THE MINISTRY, JESUS BURGERS, THAT TAKES PLACE ON FRIDAY NIGHTS IN ISLA VISTA, CALIFORNIA: WWW.JESUSBURGERS.ORG

CONTENTS

Part 3: I Will Restore to You

Part 4: The Working of Miracles

INTRODUCTION

The heartbeat and mission behind Jesus Burgers has remained the same since 2001, when the first hamburger was grilled, flipped, and sandwiched between two buns with a ketchup heart and a mustard cross. Our heart has been, and continues to be, a demonstration to the people in our community that Jesus loves them just as they are, not as they should be.

In this book, we share our ministry and some history of Jesus Burgers—stories of how people came to know Christ and got connected with this ministry. These stories are only a few of the thousands of experiences that have taken place around Jesus Burgers over the last decade as this ministry has made its impact in the city of Isla Vista.

The city of Isla Vista (often shortened to "IV" by locals) consists of more than twenty thousand people packed into less than one square mile adjacent to the University of California, Santa Barbara (UCSB). Due to the high number of college students packed into a small area, Isla Vista makes for a unique place to live or visit. Located right next to the Pacific Ocean, the area enjoys consistently sunny days and warm weather. Drivers have to yield and adapt as most people walk, skateboard, or bike to where they are going.

Apart from its picturesque location, the city of Isla Vista is infamous for its parties. Each year, UCSB ranks among the top party schools in the nation. Amplified music is allowed until midnight in the city. Students, usually drunk or high, roam the streets aimlessly searching for something to fulfill them—drugs, alcohol, and meaningless sex. And no matter what street you live on, someone is having a party.

The Jesus Burgers house has become one of those party houses. On many nights it hosts one of the biggest parties on the street. Through Jesus Burgers, Isla Vista Church (IVC) distributes around 150 hamburgers on Friday nights from our ministry house: a duplex consisting of seven guys living on the bottom floor and seven girls on the top floor. The home is located on IV's main party street: Del Playa Drive, also known as DP. This street becomes inaccessible to cars on Friday and Saturday nights as crowds of people walk up and down the street on their way to or from various parties.

Our ministry happens on Friday nights after we conclude a worship and prayer time known as the Upper Room, which takes place in the prayer shed (a converted garage behind the Jesus Burgers house). Believers fill the front yard as students walk the streets. As we start to grill, a line of people waiting for their free burgers wraps around the yard. After grabbing their burgers, people split off to rejoin their friends or sit around our fire pit and picnic table. We usually end the night sometime after one o'clock—although conversations can continue way into the morning hours.

The term "Jesus Burgers" was coined not by the IV Church but by partygoers who came each week to eat burgers. The nickname also came with "Jesus

People," which they would call those of us serving the burgers and living at the Jesus Burgers house.

We believe that both praying and loving the city tangibly through the Jesus Burgers ministry has shifted the atmosphere of the entire city in very noticeable ways. A city that was once hostile toward Christ and the Jesus Burgers ministry has come to absolutely love what God is doing. Our prayer and hope for this book is that you will see Jesus through reading about what God has done over the years in Isla Vista.

Many of the stories in this book include a lot about people's own testimonies of coming to Christ. That journey of coming to know Him is the reason why they are compelled to love others at Jesus Burgers. The stories you are about to read are stories of God's love. They are stories of how God joined His bigger story with our own stories of forgiveness, hope, and healing—stories that you can most likely relate to.

Furthermore, our hope is that in seeing Him, your hope for what is possible will increase. He is the God who showed us His love by giving His life to redeem our lives. May He convince you in your reading this book that He never gives up on people, that He loves you as you are today, and that He has a better story for each of our lives than we could possibly ask for or begin to imagine without Him.

Proverbs 18:16 says, "A gift opens the way for the giver and ushers him into the presence of the great." Jesus Burgers is a gift, a seed of love that is sown into the hearts and stomachs of people to remind us that God loves us.

Love & grace,
Jason Lomelino,
Pastor of Isla Vista Church

1

Laying Foundations

Building the Jesus Burgers Ministry

"For no other foundation can anyone lay than
that which is laid, which is Jesus Christ."

1 Corinthians 3:11 (NASB)

FATHER TO THE FATHERLESS

JASON LOMELINO

At the age of twenty-one, I had a radical encounter with God in which I heard Him audibly ask the question, "What are you living for, Jason?" From that moment on, my life has been forever messed up, in the best possible way. It was the first time in my life that I felt free! Free from false comforts and identities, and free to be who God created me to be. I can't describe the feeling in words, but I knew that I knew that I knew that Jesus was real and God was the author of the peace and love I had been looking for my whole life.

I came to Christ from a background of alcohol and drugs and doing whatever I wanted to do. The good news of forgiveness and instant freedom from enslaving habits opened my eyes to new life in a way I could never have imagined. Within a week of giving my life to Christ, God brought me to Isla Vista to connect me with other believers. By that first week, it had become clear to me that God was sending me to IV to tell my generation the most amazing news I had ever heard—the good news that Jesus Christ loves them and is alive today!

A few months later, I heard God speak to me again, asking me to rally as many people in the city to put on a barbecue at Anisq' Oyo' Park, which is located in the center of downtown Isla Vista. God said, "Play music at the barbecue and share about Me." This barbecue brought in about a hundred people and marked the beginning of the Jesus Burgers ministry. We ended up serving Jesus Burgers once a month for about four months, eventually moving the ministry to Del Playa Drive at the Jesus Burger house.

For my wife and me, Isla Vista has become a modern day Promise Land, although many people in Santa Barbara would associate it more with Sodom and Gomorrah. God has been at work in this city, and the atmosphere is notably different from when we moved here in 2001. Back then, every Friday and Saturday night was characterized by fights, couch burnings, a sense of recklessness, and incredible spiritual oppression. It was so oppressive that when believers would come out on Friday nights to walk up and down Del Playa to pray and tell people about Jesus, they would often become nauseated or suddenly begin to experience intense headaches. There was no natural reason for these reactions aside from demonic opposition in the spiritual realm.

When we first started Jesus Burgers, there was no ministry house on Del Playa (the residence now known as the Jesus Burgers house); we had no home base, so we would find ourselves just walking up and down the street like everyone else. We would interrupt groups of students and ask a simple question like, "What do you think about Jesus?" To our astonishment, we frequently found that in a circle of three to six people most of them were receptive to talking with us. We would begin to share about Christ, but almost always someone in the group would steer the entire group away. These days were epic, as they required great risk and faith; we never knew if people were going to hate us for our witness or be open to conversing with us.

I can remember getting into some of the funniest conversations in these early days, as I was so young in the Lord and didn't really know what I was doing besides sharing about the hope that I had found in Jesus Christ.

One time I overheard some guys talking about the desire to get high, so I immediately jumped in and said, "I heard you guys want to get high? Well, I have something that will blow your mind, that you will never come down from, and that will mess your life up forever." Because I said this with so much genuine joy and excitement, I had a captive audience; even a few others who were standing around us had heard me say this and leaned in to listen.

I waited a few seconds to build anticipation and finally blurted out, "It's Jesus!" Surprisingly the guys just laughed at me and told me in a joking manner to "get out of here." Nevertheless, I ended up having a ridiculously good conversation with these guys, sharing my whole testimony of how I came to Christ, how He delivered me from alcohol and drugs, and how life in God is the only thing that satisfies.

In the early years, giving away Jesus Burgers was nothing like it is today. In 2002, when we first began serving the hamburgers on Del Playa, the infamous party street, our burgers were not readily received. People would accuse us from time to time of poisoning the food or trying to use the burgers to convert them. The atmosphere was very different then, even though the message of unconditional love and acceptance has always been the same.

This situation continued for the first few years

until God began changing IV both in the seen and unseen—opening people's eyes to the blessing that Jesus Burgers was to the city. I distinctly remember one Friday night in 2005, when a fight was about to break out in the front yard of our house. This was something that had happened several times before; however, this time people in the crowd began shouting, "Hey, hey, we're at the Jesus Burgers house. Stop that right now. That is not cool, bro. Jesus loves us and these people love us." And sure enough the fight was diffused! To this day, I can't remember the last time a fight broke out on our property.

The Jesus Burgers house has become a house of peace for the city. We usually have a small bonfire going on in the front yard where people can hang out and warm themselves; women are sometimes dressed for tropical weather when they should be wearing their winter clothes! Nevertheless, God's presence is real in this place; whether or not you are a believer, His supernatural peace is undeniable on the property of the Jesus Burgers house. I cannot tell you how many times people have walked into the front of the house, not even knowing where they were, and have said in their own language, "What the F, this place is so peaceful."

I remember one time being in front of the house thanking God for the peace that He had given us, when suddenly this guy with a bicked head, tank top, and tattoos stopped in the middle of the street right in front of the house. I knew as soon as I saw him that God had a word for Him; I felt overcome by the love of God for this person I had never met. Feeling the unconditional love of God for someone has always been a great indicator that God wants me to get involved with what He is doing in someone's life. So without thinking much about it, I walked up to the guy, thinking that God would give me something to share with him when I got there. However, to my dismay, I had nothing when I got to him besides the cliché "God loves you."

Most people just say thanks or ignore it when you say that, but this guy looked at me with almost rage in his eyes, clenched his fists, and said in a stern voice, "What did you say?" Thinking I was going to get socked for the name of Jesus, I replied in perfect peace, "God loves you." He instantly shot back, "Why did you tell me that? Why!? Tell me right now why you said that to me!!!"

I replied, "Because I looked over at you and was instantly overcome by God's love for you." What happened next caught me off guard more than everything else leading up to this point. Just as I was thinking this guy was done with me and that a beat down for Jesus was on the way, he grabbed me and squeezed me tighter than any man with big arms and tattoos should squeeze someone who is obviously not built the same way. But what he said into my ear after a few seconds of holding me was something I will never forget: he muttered, "I was planning on taking my life tonight thinking that nobody loves me and there is no God."

After he said these words, he began crying in my arms in the middle of the street, not letting me go. It felt like at least five minutes, but it was probably a lot shorter. After I was freed from the hulk's arms, I shared with him the hope found in Christ and the love of God demonstrated for him on the cross. We did not have time for a long conversation on the street as his buddies were inside the yard getting Jesus Burgers; but that night, like so many others, changed one person's life for eternity—in just a moment's time. God is good, always.

My wife, Holly, and I have lived in IV for more than ten years now. We could not be more thankful to live in this city and raise our family here. Along with others, we helped plant the Isla Vista Church in 2002, and I became the lead pastor in 2007. In 2005, Holly and I moved into a community house with twenty-plus people for two and a half years, functioning as the house dad and mom. Our son Samuel was one month old when we moved into this community house we referred to as "Shiloh." Our beautiful daughter Hope was also born during the time we lived at Shiloh.

My wife and I still live in Isla Vista with our four kids, our dog, and our many spiritual children. We have no plans to move anywhere else, for we believe God sent us to this city even before we met each other. I believe strongly that God desires each of our lives to become the message we preach. What my wife and I have been called to do by living in a college town, raising our kids here, and believing God for a generation to know Christ, is what we believe many other families will be doing in the years to come.

College campuses are the mind molders that influence the next generation of world leaders. Just as my wife Holly and I have fathered and mothered others, God is raising up others to serve as spiritual fathers and mothers to plant roots in college towns throughout the United States—living lives that are easily accessible to others, allowing for God to grow a family in the midst of an orphan-minded generation.

We strongly believe that the church was meant to be a family, not a place you go to only once a week. The Bible actually says "God sets the lonely in families" (Psalm 68:6), not church buildings. I want to be clear that we are not at all against church, as I had a supernatural experience in 2007, when an angel showed up in my room during one of the harder seasons of my life, after I had asked the question out loud to God, "What am I doing, God?" I then heard the angel respond audibly, "You are planting a church in IV." Little did I know then what God had planned for His church in Isla Vista!

Jesus Burgers is all about love; it's about the love of God being demonstrated through His people. There is nothing fancy about this ministry. It is merely a bunch of people who have been radically arrested by God's love, showing that same love to others through a hamburger, a glass of water, a walk home, an encouraging word, a conversation, or a simple prayer.

I have countless stories from these nights, stories that would blow most people away: stories of people telling me things that they've never shared with anyone, stories of people crying in my arms, stories of hope, stories of redemption, stories that have not yet been written in history, but each and every one of which the Father already knows. Yes, each story reflects the intimate concern and care of a Father who created His children to know Him and be loved by Him.

We live in a day and hour when people want the most out of life with the least amount of commitment. God isn't like that. He is a committed Father, and He will do whatever it takes to bring his lost children home. We believe God is calling His people to commit, to leave the comfort of the church, and to love others simply where they are in life. That is why, after a decade, we are still involved with the Jesus Burgers ministry. We are so thankful for Jesus Burgers and the seeds of love it has sown into many lives—seeds that would not have been sown apart from the faithfulness of God. Jesus alone is the hope of the nations, and our hope is that He will be made famous in Isla Vista, and beyond.

How Do You Reach a City? How Do You Reach a Generation?

Holly Lomelino

I came to know Jesus as my personal Lord and Savior as a child. I grew up in a home that was at first just culturally Christian, in the Bible belt of America, the Midwest. Our family claimed to be Christians, attending church mostly only at Christmas and Easter. After I started asking my family to take me to church on Sundays and started hungering to really know God, I began learning how much it wasn't about church or what you did or didn't do—it was about faith and a genuine relationship with Jesus.

When I gave Him my life and trusted Him as my Savior, I began the greatest adventure I could ever know. He has taken me from a lonely, depressed, and sometimes even suicidal child to a free, joyful, life-loving adult. The joy, hope, and love I've experienced in my over twenty years of walking with Jesus is indescribable. I can't imagine my life without Him, and can honestly say He is the best thing that has ever happened to me. Jesus has saved me and healed me in more ways than I can count.

My journey with God in Isla Vista actually began in Africa. It was 1998, and I was on a mission trip to

Zimbabwe the summer before I went off to Westmont College, the Christian college in Santa Barbara. It was during our debriefing at the end of the trip that the Lord spoke to me and told me that I was going to attend Westmont, but my ministry would be at UC Santa Barbara. I had no idea what that would mean or what the ministry would look like, but I believed Him and received it.

The week I arrived at Westmont, I saw a sign advertising a Westmont campus ministry involved in discipleship and evangelism at UCSB. I was in. I joined the ministry and came out every Friday to UCSB. We walked around campus, got into conversations with students, and shared the good news about Jesus with those we encountered. We also had weekly prayer meetings for the university campus.

God was beginning to give me an even greater heart for UCSB. He was also beginning to give me promises for the campus and city of Isla Vista that were mind-blowing: thousands of students coming to Jesus and seeing Del Playa filled with people worshiping God instead of drunk and partying.

The next year, my sophomore year, I became the leader of that ministry, and my heart began to grow and break even more for UCSB and IV. I was seeing my peers, my own generation, searching so desperately for love and significance, for a reason to live, and for something to believe in. It didn't take long for me to ask God how to reach a city and how to reach this generation of youth that were so desperately in need of love and a Savior. God was faithful to give me revelation as I sought His will.

One night, He spoke to me very clearly from John 13:35, "By this everyone will know that you are my disciples, if you love one another." He showed me that when the Body of Christ begins to love radically, live radically, and be the Body of Christ He intended, the lost will be reached and thousands will be saved.

It was not enough to have only one or two believers focus on the lost. We needed a radical community of believers loving one another supernaturally and loving the city with that same love. Only then could a whole city be saved. Little did I know, that revelation was the beginning of a long journey that led to the birth of Isla Vista Church.

At the end of that year, God spoke to me from 1 Thessalonians 2:8 where Paul says, "Having so fond an affection for you, we were well-pleased to impart to you not only the gospel of God but also our own lives, because you had become very dear to us." Isla Vista had become so dear to me that I knew I needed to share not only the Gospel with the city but my life as well.

I was being called to move to Isla Vista. I knew that my impact was limited by only going there once a week. I needed to be in IV all of the time to really build relationships and have a greater influence. Even though it gave me a twenty-seven-mile commute to school, I moved out of the Westmont dorms and into a duplex in the city of Isla Vista my junior year.

Living in IV, I fell in love with the city even more. My heart began to burn with a passion to see the youth of the city come to know their Maker. Day and night, I couldn't stop thinking about it, and I couldn't stop wondering how the people could come to know Him. Since I didn't know how to make this happen, I spent a lot of time on my face crying out to God for Him to do it.

My friend Robin Hulett (who lived across the street) and I would get up each morning at six o'clock to pray for IV. God challenged us with this at the beginning of that school year. While it was a bit of a sacrifice to get up and do this each day, it was totally worth it. God met us in those early morning prayer times and continued to grow in us a heart to see IV redeemed. Those prayer times quickly turned into action, and we started inviting neighbors to weekly dinners at our home. We wanted to love the people of IV and begin to engage them in authentic relationships.

Once I was living in Isla Vista, I quickly realized that there was a Christian "bubble" not only at Westmont but even at UC Santa Barbara. There seemed to be a clear divide between the Christians and the rest of the world. I knew we could never reach those we could not touch. If we didn't start sharing our lives with them, inviting them into our world, and going out to join theirs, we would never be able to touch them with the love of Christ. The dinners we hosted were our first attempt at breaking down this divide. I love how this was a prophetic foreshadowing of what was to eventually come through Jesus Burgers. Feeding people is such a practical and tangible way to love them!

God also used these dinners to bring me Jason, my husband—the person who would carry the vision of Isla Vista with me. During the time I was studying abroad in Kenya (spring semester 2001), Jason Lomelino came to know Jesus and was brought out to Isla Vista to one of the dinners at my house. He connected with my roommates, and when I returned to California at the end of the semester, we became instant friends. Jason and I found in one another a heart and a passion for IV that matched. At first we were just excited to work together doing community barbecues. Little did we know this would be the catalyst to our relationship and our continued ministry in Isla Vista as leaders and pastors!

Another really significant thing that happened

the year I moved out to Isla Vista was that God put it on my heart to organize a week of 24-7 prayer during fall 2000. This meant finding enough people to pray for Isla Vista twenty-four hours a day for a full week. I was so desperate for God to come move in Isla Vista, and I knew prayer was the key.

Robin and I created a stack of signup lists and passed them out to everyone we could—friends, campus ministry groups, and different churches in town. We wanted believers all over Santa Barbara to join us in this prayer effort. Finally, we had almost all of the 168 time slots filled. I was so excited and had no idea what God was going to do during this week of prayer for Isla Vista! I emailed and called people to make sure they remembered to pray during their chosen hour, and I took the hours no one had signed up for, or found others who would. That week I think there was more intercession going up for Isla Vista than ever before! I had no doubt God was going to move through those hundreds of prayers!

One of the most significant results of that week happened when a young couple named Jacob and Kimberly Reeve signed up for one hour. During that time of praying for Isla Vista, God did a radical work in their hearts, taking them from a strong dislike of IV to a newfound passion for the city.

Soon after, Jacob contacted me about wanting to do more in Isla Vista. I was about to go to Kenya to study abroad for a semester, so I told him I couldn't really do much at that point. He decided to start a prayer meeting at his home, and his own story tells of the incredible journey God took him on from there. But ultimately, it led to Jacob getting the Jesus Burgers house and then starting Isla Vista Church, the community of believers that would eventually carry the earlier keys to reaching a city God had given me two years before.

I am continuously amazed at the goodness and faithfulness of God. When I first came out to Isla Vista I thought I would only be around for a few years, like most college students. Now, there is nowhere else in the world I would rather be. I love getting to see Him transform the lives of college students through meeting them right where they are and sharing love and a burger with them. And I love getting to see a city transformed, one life at a time.

A HOUSE
HOLY UNTO
HIM

JACOB REEVE

In 2000, my wife, Kim, and I regularly attended the college group of Calvary Chapel Santa Barbara called Reality. One Friday night at Reality, Holly Lomelino, a Westmont College student, and Robin Hulett, a University of California, Santa Barbara, student, sent around a clipboard with timeslots to sign up for a week of prayer for Isla Vista.

Saying yes to helping out with the prayer needs was one of those things I felt obligated to do because of the church's emotional plea of the moment. At the time, I didn't really care too much for Isla Vista. Nevertheless, my wife and I signed up for the 3:00–4:00 a.m. slot.

We talked about it on the way home, and I said, "How are we going to pray for an hour for Isla Vista? I hate IV."

Despite our reservations, we were faithful in setting our alarm to wake up to pray. We couldn't have guessed what would happen as a result of those first prayers for Isla Vista. In that hour of prayer, my wife and I had seen God's heart for IV. That prayer time gave us enough grace to channel every bit of life and love we had toward the people and town of Isla Vista for the next seven years.

A few weeks later, a really big south swell was hitting the coast of California. I had a free pass to the military base to surf some of the best waves in the state. At the time, I was a professional bodyboarder, and that day I had plans to meet a videographer and photographer at the base to take pictures for my sponsors.

The night before, I had an encounter with God, who called me up to the mountains to fast and pray. I had never heard God say much to me before that night. I called my friends to tell them I wasn't coming because God was calling me to fast and pray. They thought I was crazy. I said it then, and I stand by it now: I would rather be crazy with God than in my right mind without Him.

I drove up old San Marcos Road and found a place to sit and pray. Less than five minutes later a vision appeared in which I saw a before-and-after scene of Isla Vista. The before scene showed me the city under its current government of spiritual darkness. The after scene showed me how IV would look if it came under the government of God. The parties had not ended, but the partiers were changed—they had been redeemed. Instead of seeing depressed and empty partiers who were drunk on beer, I saw thousands of people worshiping God in love—drunk on the ecstasy of the presence of the Holy Spirit.

God slowly showed me face after face, like a slideshow. It seemed like a thousand faces of young partiers from Del Playa Drive flashed before my eyes.

I heard a voice say, "How could you not?"

I knew immediately what that meant. If I didn't do something for them, no one else would. How could I not act?

When I told my wife, Kim, about this experience,

she was cut to the heart. We hugged each other and prayed for the fulfillment of God's Kingdom in Isla Vista. We began a Monday night prayer meeting at our house. Britt Merrick, the Reality college pastor, had already been diligently praying for Isla Vista, and he was happy to hear that others had caught the vision. He let me make an announcement at Reality. By the next prayer meeting, we had four others join us: Ashley, Luke, Mark, and Graham.

We didn't know what we were doing—we knew only that we had to pray. Our group remained small, but to this day, I have not seen a prayer meeting more productive than those early ones. It seemed as though every prayer we prayed was answered within a week.

At the time, it seemed like the church body of Santa Barbara had almost completely forsaken Isla Vista. It was as if Isla Vista was Goliath. Everyone we talked to would say something like, "IV is going to hell" or "IV is Sodom and Gomorrah" or "IV is a pastor's graveyard." These were all intimidating statements, but praise God that Christ had compelled us to believe a better report.

We figured that Isla Vista was so dark that if we could get in and host a corporate worship time, it would surely displace the darkness! Over the course of a year, we ended up hosting four worship nights at a park in downtown Isla Vista. We invited churches across Santa Barbara to join us.

A year prior to this, my wife and I had started a skateboard ministry at the local skate park. We would bring a grill to the park every Thursday night and barbecue food for the local skate kids. God showed us that hospitality has always been a major part of church life and that food was a great tool in the ministry of reconciliation.

Based on our skateboard ministry, we felt convinced that we ought to have food at the first worship night, but we did not have the budget for that, so we prayed. Within the week, Robin Hulett and Jason Lomelino got in contact with us and asked if we wanted them to barbecue for the event! They also offered to pass out flyers throughout the city to raise awareness for the event. All our needs for the ministry were being met through prayer! This series of events laid the foundation for the Jesus Burgers ministry.

After the fourth and final worship night, a few of us decided to walk down Del Playa to the epicenter of the parties. As we walked, the Lord showed me His heart for that street. He wanted to move in.

We began regular prayer-walking on Del Playa each weekend. This activity quickly became prayer-evangelism, for as we would be praying and mingling with the crowd, students would approach us for sex or drugs. We responded quickly, "No way!" Then the partiers would ask what we were doing, and we would tell them we were praying. "What?!" was the usual response.

Once we presented the Gospel to them, bizarre things would happen. We encountered a lot of threats and witnessed outbursts of anger against God and others. Our group didn't behave very maturely in those early days. All we had was love and hope. As it turns out, love and hope are all you need.

Kim and I were convinced God would have us move to IV with our family. We began praying for a permanent house in Isla Vista. God highlighted four houses to me and gave me a promise. Two of them were across from a little park with a view of the ocean and a short walk to the beach access. The others were down the street closer to campus.

For a few months, I drove out to Isla Vista every week and prayed over these houses, asking God to give them to us. We waited patiently, but many weeks passed, and Kim and I did not receive what we knew the Lord had promised us.

My faith felt crushed. It was difficult to keep praying, but we did. My daily thought sustained me, that we "through faith and patience inherit the promises" (Hebrews 6:12).

For the next six months, a group of us from Reality continued prayer-walking in the streets during weekend parties. Finally, I heard God speak to me again about the four addresses.

"I am giving you that house," He would say. What house? I'd ask in my head.

I felt God had let me down the time before, so I did not want to believe Him. But this time He added, "for the church family."

Then it made sense. If God had given the house to me earlier, I would have moved in with my wife and kids. Instead, God wanted a community of students living together on Del Playa.

I told Britt Merrick about this conviction and asked him to pray. I met with the management companies and discovered that two of them had already been rented and the third one required six thousand dollars up front just to get on the waiting list!

I did not have faith for that kind of money. I went across the street from 6686 Del Playa Drive. It was the only property of the four God had showed me whose details and owner remained unknown. For all I knew, it was already rented. I stared at the property, hanging onto hope and praying for God to work.

His promise came to me again, "I am giving you this house."

I decided to anoint the house with oil as an act of faith. I was in the process of smearing the back corner when the drug-dealing tenants caught me on their property. A shady guy opened the back sliding door.

"What are you doing, bro?" he asked.

"I am anointing your house with oil."

"Oh," he said, closing the door. Whew! I kept on, a smile forming across my face. They didn't know the power in what I was doing!

I hopped on the freeway back to Calvary Chapel Santa Barbara to see if I could find someone to pray with me for the property. When I arrived, I went through the main sanctuary instead of the front office. Britt spotted me from across the room.

"Hey, Jacob! Any news on getting an apartment on Del Playa?"

Some guy out in the hall overhead us and yelled, "Are you looking for an apartment on Del Playa?" In walked a man named Jason Cox. I told him that I was.

"I'm an apartment manager in Isla Vista. I have an apartment at 6686 Del Playa that I was about to put up for lease. Do you want it?"

That was the beginning of the Jesus Burgers house.

God is amazing and His word is true. What if Kim and I had given up a year before when I felt I had been let down? What then? Like His Word says, we will "through FAITH and PATIENCE inherit the promises!" (Hebrews 6:12).

The next year twelve young believers moved in. We planted the new church that September (2002), and I became the pastor. We served Jesus Burgers on Saturday nights and met for Sunday services in the front yard.

Originally, our lease gave us access to the apartment only, not the detached two-car garage behind it. Jim, the owner of the property, used the garage for storage.

About a year after our church began to lease the house, a group of us went to the Goleta Valley Healing Rooms hosted by our pastor friends from the local Vineyard Church.

During that time, I had a revelation about a house of prayer in Isla Vista on Del Playa Drive. I asked Derika, Brian, Jason, and Holly to pray with me that Jim would allow us to use the garage behind the Jesus Burgers house. I remember praying and coming into agreement with everyone that if God would give us that back garage, we would consecrate it and make it holy unto Him. It would be used only for His Kingdom and for prayer.

I had not spoken to Jim about the garage since we had first rented the property. Since then I had only spoken to Jim a total of three or four times.

I returned from the healing rooms at around nine o'clock that night. An hour later, I was in bed when the phone rang. It was Jim.

"Jacob! I was getting ready for bed, and I began thinking that you really deserve that garage in back of the house."

I screamed into the phone, "WE JUST PRAYED YOU WOULD GIVE THAT TO US!"

"Yeah, you should have that place," he said. "I'll come this next week and clear out all my stuff."

"How much?" I asked.

"No, it's yours. You deserve it. I like you guys." Then he asked me if he could take me out to dinner. He had questions about church and God. Amazing!

God's love is so much bigger and greater than we could ever imagine. He loved Isla Vista way before my wife and I wanted to step foot in the place. He gave us His heart for Isla Vista, and He ordered our steps. He paved the way for us to start a church and cultivate a ministry that would communicate His heart to the city. He is faithful, and if we will believe and stay our ground, He will accomplish what He has promised. His story in IV has only just begun, and it's about to get a whole lot more glorious!

GIFT OF GOD

DERIKA SIMS

W hen we served the first Jesus Burger on Del Playa Drive, I was twenty-one years old and my name was Derika Brendsel. The name Derika (rhymes with Erika) means "ruler of the people." Most of my school years were spent in Montana where I was raised by incredible parents. I came to faith in high school and followed God's call to attend Westmont College in Santa Barbara, California.

At age sixteen, I started wearing a silver purity ring on my left hand. The ring served as a visual reminder of my commitment to remain sexually abstinent until marriage. The first time I put it on, a Scripture from Matthew's gospel popped into my head: "Blessed are the pure in heart, for they shall see God." I treasured this verse throughout my college years, praying often that others would see Jesus in me.

When I first began prayer-walking in Isla Vista, I was a fish out of water. I had lived on a Christian campus for four years and was not accustomed to seeing capable young people casting off restraint in the middle of the street. From public make-out sessions to smoking pot on the sidewalk to hundreds of underage students drinking every weekend, it was eye-opening. When our ministry acquired the Jesus Burgers house and started the church, I didn't want to be anywhere else.

In Isla Vista, the biggest street party of the year falls on Halloween weekend. The first Halloween we served Jesus Burgers was in 2002. I marveled at the sea of humanity pouring down Del Playa Drive. Since my birthday is also on Halloween, I was accustomed to costume parties, but never an entire city at once! Guys from our church set up a giant grill in the front yard, and we made an incredible assembly line for the buns and condiments.

We served a thousand people that weekend. My friend Brian and I met a student named Rasheed who came from a Rastafarian background. We invited him upstairs and talked with him for over three hours. At the end of the night, Rasheed sketched a picture for me as a way of saying thanks. The friendship that grew out of that first conversation continued for years as he would come back to the house to talk about issues in his life.

At Jesus Burgers, I felt God's presence in the midst of my conversations. At first, students seemed aloof, arrogant, or downright antagonistic. But we kept praying, and God gave us courage to persevere. I learned to listen—both to the Holy Spirit and the students—and I began to see laughter, tears, and a hunger for the truth. God's love was breaking through hardened hearts.

More than sermons or Bible studies or even times of worship, encounters at Jesus Burgers made me feel alive, purposeful, and focused on the ministry of reconciliation. It was exhilarating.

The Isla Vista variety of relationships are often characterized by alcohol, sex, betrayal, and pain. "I like girls too much to seek God" is a comment I've heard more than once. With a shrug of their shoulders, bold young men tell me the pleasures of sin are too enticing to consider God's plan.

One night, I introduced myself to a slender brunette as I served her a hamburger. She told me her name was Katherine. "Do you know what your name means?" I asked. She didn't.

"Pure" I said, smiling. Her face fell, eyes filling with pain.

"Katherine means pure, but I'm not pure," she said softly. I took time to minister to her with the love of God and speak words of encouragement and compassion. She asked for my number, completely blown away. "This girl is speaking words I need to hear," she told the others in the line.

On another night, I shared about salvation by grace with a quiet Catholic named Mark. Halfway into our discussion Mark told me he was gay. I explained that everyone is in need of forgiveness, gay and straight alike. Christ's blood was shed for all to be saved. He gave me a hug and thanked me for being the first Christian he had ever met who learned his orientation and still spoke to him about Jesus with dignity and respect.

Most of the time my singleness didn't bother me. Trusting God was not easy, but I knew it was worth it. When appropriate, I shared my story to encourage others: I was a virgin, and even though my friends were starting families, I was still trusting God to bring me a husband. In the meantime, I enjoyed friendships with my brothers in Christ and stayed committed to ministry in Isla Vista. In 2006, I started a blog of real-life testimonies from my experiences at Jesus Burgers.

Because I was still single, some of my friends

urged me to change churches, sign up for a dating website, or stop wearing my purity ring because it might discourage potential suitors. I understood their rationale; I was closer to thirty than twenty, and the single men at my church were young college students.

Seven years after that first Halloween Jesus Burgers, I was preparing for another intense weekend of outreach. It was October 2009, and I was living in IV, right around the corner from Jason and Holly Lomelino. I slung my Nikon over my shoulder, intending to snap some shots for my blog, and walked the seven cold blocks to the ministry house.

A normal night of Jesus Burgers allows for a lot of conversations. Halloween is another story. The sheer number of people, the sirens from emergency vehicles, and the general clamor make it difficult to stand outside and speak to anyone. Think of trying to share your testimony in a mosh pit.

I climbed onto the three-foot wall around the yard to get a better view. The multitudes were pouring down the street, searching for friends, flings, and fun. Nearly everyone was wearing a costume and trying to be noticed. They were sheep without a shepherd.

An hour later, I saw a dark-haired guy wearing a fedora hat and standing on the wall. Was he a student searching for his friends or a Christian from one of the campus ministries? I couldn't tell.

"Nice view up there, huh?" I said, giving him a friendly smile.

He agreed but said nothing else. It was too loud and too awkward to pursue a conversation from the ground, so I left it at that. I spent the rest of the night praying, picking up trash, greeting visitors, and caring for students who had passed out.

Well after midnight, I reached into my jacket pocket and pulled out my cell phone to check the time. It was officially October 31st, the wee hours of Halloween morning. I smiled, giving myself an internal Happy Birthday.

The Millers, a middle-aged couple involved in campus ministry, were visiting Isla Vista that weekend. I met the Millers years before when they first visited IV from Hollywood. On this trip, they brought someone new. I was surprised to see it was the guy who had been standing on the wall.

"Hello," he said, "I'm Nathanael." Our ice-cold hands met for a handshake as the Millers introduced me. Nathanael is a Biblical name, and I wondered what it meant. I asked if he knew.

Nathanael began to shake his head but then paused, unsure.

"Well," he said, "according to the plaque on the wall of my childhood bedroom, Nathanael means 'gift of God.'"

Being the birthday girl, that caught my attention!

Nathanael had only met the Millers that day and had never been to Jesus Burgers before. He asked me some questions about the ministry's history, and I gave him an overview.

The next night in the prayer shed (the evening of October 31), we had just finished our time of worship and prayer when Pastor Jason Lomelino stood to address the group.

"It's Derika's birthday today!" he announced. "I want to take a moment to honor Derika for her faithfulness to Jesus Burgers and her partnership in ministry with me and Holly."

I squirmed in my seat, embarrassed but flattered. Nearby, Nathanael listened with interest. Just a few nights before, Nathanael felt the Holy Spirit prompting him to write a list of the qualities he wanted in a wife. As Jason gave a generous description of my character and gifts, Nathanael noted that I fit the list.

A few hours later, as the burgers were being served, a stranger smashed a large bottle at the foot of the driveway. The shattered bits lay sharp and menacing in the darkness. I ran to grab a cardboard box. When I returned, Nathanael was crouching over the mess, his hands full of broken glass he had already gathered.

"Here, Nate, use this." I thrust the box toward him as he looked up, surprised. (I hadn't asked if I could call him Nate, it just came out.) We made quick work of the mess. I tossed the box in the dumpster, and we parted ways.

At the end of the night, I leaned against the wall of the house, bone-tired but content. A few believers grabbed a guitar and began singing worship songs around the dwindling fire.

"So, I hear you're a screenwriter." I looked to my right, surprised to see Nathanael standing nearby.

At the time, I was working on a screenplay about a teenage boy who gets adopted out of foster care. My background was in writing, not in film, but I had become increasingly interested in film production.

Nathanael told me he was an independent filmmaker. We struck up a conversation in the front yard that outlasted even the late crowd. I did most of the talking, Nathanael's exceptional listening skills drawing out more than I would normally share with a newcomer.

For years, I had been listening to the stories of the students who came to Jesus Burgers. I had prayed with them, shared about salvation in Jesus, and listened to their perspective on spirituality. No stranger had ever come to Jesus Burgers to listen to me. I was thankful, but when Nathanael left with the Millers the next evening, I did not expect to see him again.

A few days later, I opened my email account to find a lengthy message from Nathanael Sims. We had not exchanged contact information but he had found my Jesus Burgers blog online. Nathanael and I emailed back and forth for a few weeks and met for breakfast when I was in his area visiting a friend.

One of my greatest fears about marriage was that I might have to move away from the ministry I had devoted the last decade of my life to building. After serving with Jacob and Kimberly Reeve and then Jason and Holly Lomelino for so long, I could not bear saying goodbye forever. Not long after Nathanael and I became friends, he started visiting Isla Vista to see me and attend Jesus Burgers and church.

Without knowing about the list, I managed to fulfill all of the qualities he was seeking in a wife. Including #39: She MUST be my age. Nathanael was twenty-nine years old when he came to Jesus Burgers for Halloween weekend and met me on my birthday. I had been twenty-nine for about an hour.

How's that for a divine appointment?

Today, Nathanael and I use our film production skills to make videos of baptisms, testimonies, and worship sessions. We have one completed feature film and plans for more. Married couples at Jesus Burgers are rare. We are thankful to be involved, testifying of God's love and grace, and telling the story of how he used Jesus Burgers to bring us together.

A City Changed from Chaos to Light

MARILYNN GRANADO

I was just a small thing, only three years old, when I accepted Jesus into my heart. I grew up in a Christian home and knew at that young age that I was a sinner and needed forgiveness.

I got involved in Isla Vista around 1999–2000. Though I became involved in a college ministry that was vibrant, I felt frustrated that the people of God were not reaching a whole city full of college students. I used to meet with two guys and pray for Isla Vista on a regular basis, but we soon grew frustrated because we did not have a tangible way to tell people about the love of God other than inviting them to church or a college group.

I noticed a town full of lawlessness, where drunkenness was celebrated. I felt the need to tell these people that life was more than getting to the next high, whether that be with sex, drugs, or alcohol. I saw the aching hole in a city that was desperately ignorant of God. It was a city of kids without a Father. Our group wanted a way to reach a large portion of the residents, but we could not invite hundreds of people over to a house to hang out. Since IV was known for large house parties on the weekends, we decided to have a party of our own. We invited our worship band, bought a root beer keg, and hoped people would show up. The police shut us down very soon after we started because we were on Sabado Tarde. Although this street was just one below Del Playa (the main party street), the noise ordinance started at ten o'clock instead of midnight.

Since having our own "party" did not work, we thought being in a common area would allow us to gather people to us. Our college group started to go out to Anisq' Oyo' Park in IV to worship, preach a gospel message, and feed whoever was there. We did this for a while—but in our minds, the times at the park were infrequent at best, and the majority of the students we wanted to reach weren't coming. Although these gatherings were geared for the masses, they ended up drawing Christians (most of whom were starved for other believers in a sometimes hostile city) but very few unsaved. We knew we needed to be in the midst of the people instead of trying to drag them to us. To reach these people, we needed to live among them.

When I reflect on my time with Jesus Burgers, the words that come to mind are "community change." It is funny to think about now, but when we started, people wouldn't take the burgers: some thought they were poisoned; many did not want to wait in line.

A palpable, heavy spiritual darkness cloaked the whole square mile; intoxicated, swearing, verbally abusive people crowded the streets. When I first started going into IV, it was so spiritually dark that I would feel a physical heaviness settle over me when I drove in. I would get concentrated headaches and fatiguing nausea when my car hit El Colegio, the street bordering the city. During most nights, furniture was set on fire, men and women were unable to walk straight, people vomited and peed on our property, and fights erupted. I remember fistfights breaking out inside our home. In a word it was chaos.

During Halloween, I could not drive close to IV. I would pray from another location just because I could not handle being in the city due to the demonic playground it became that weekend.

Now the spiritual atmosphere is infused with light. In fact, people who wait in line for a burger are almost always thankful instead of suspicious. Now people know our house, and that they can come and get help if there is illness or they are lost.

One encounter of change happened to me as I was out on the streets. I used to go out and prayer-walk the streets, praying peace, purity, and freedom over the people. One of my favorite times was in 2007. I was out praying when a guy on the street yelled to me and my friends that we should go get a burger at the Jesus Burgers house. I asked why, and he told me that the burgers were good. I told him that it could not be that good, and he explained that the best part was that God was there and we should check it out. That was pretty rich. Here was a complete stranger telling me about Jesus Burgers, and the one thing he wanted me to know was that God was there. How amazing to think that this was the same city that I could not even come into a few years earlier, and now I was being told to find out about God by a complete stranger. What a change!

I have seen other evidence of change in the community over the years. Before, fights used to draw massive crowds of cheering spectators who egged on the fighters; but the change happened around 2008–09; we actually had people on the street who were not connected with us that stopped people who were fighting because they were fighting in front of the Jesus Burgers house. Who would have guessed that just being consistent in loving people would cause such a change in the overall atmosphere? The students of IV were choosing peace instead of violence.

My heart is for the Jesus Burgers house to be the best party house on the street—a party house directed toward life-giving, not mind-numbing, pursuits. I do not believe that the party atmosphere in Isla Vista is wrong; it is just focused in the wrong direction. I would love for the people of Isla Vista to know how valuable they are and that they are loved beyond words. That is why we give away burgers. It is easier to give away food to show your love than to try and give a stranger a hug. In the end that is truly my heart: that the people in Isla Vista know that God loves them right in the middle of their lives. He is pursuing them, and so, as His people, we are too.

For those who are reading this and want to start your own ministry, know that we were not wildly successful at the beginning. In fact, I think only after year seven did we start having success and seeing fruit that was tangible. I am not saying that there was not fruit before, but we were not told about testimonies until sometimes years later. The second thing I would say is that you cannot go out to do Jesus Burgers. It is a great idea, but the idea is not the reason for success; Jesus Burgers has succeeded because the Lord's Spirit enabled it. My suggestion is to ask the Lord how to reach your community in a practical way, and then discipline yourself to do it, even when you don't feel like it.

If anything, I think Jesus Burgers—a tiny ministry in a tiny town—has become known because we had not "despised the days of small things" (Zechariah 4:10).

2

The Plans I Have for You

Dedicating One's Life to Jesus

" 'For I know the plans I have for you,' declares
the Lord, 'plans to prosper you and not to harm
you, plans to give you hope and a future.' "

—JEREMIAH 29:11 (NIV)

COMING FULL CIRCLE

AVA AMES

When I was a little girl, I had all the humor and personality in the world to put a smile on anyone's face. I was true to who I was: a go-getting, spunky girl who saw the good in everyone. But life inevitably took a few unexpected turns, and I was forced to learn challenging lessons at a young age. The difficult times in my life were characterized by divorce, abandonment, and abuse. It wasn't easy dealing with these things, but I made the most out of my situation and was determined to create a world for myself that I defined. In high school, I had an upbeat, respectable reputation and received good grades. I tried not to deal with the pain I felt inside while growing up, since it was far easier for me to ignore it and bottle it up.

However, throughout my life, I never let go of my relationship with God. I knew He desired love for my life, and I held on to the belief that Jesus died for my sins. Some years I pictured Him thousands of feet in the sky, distant and preoccupied. And other years, I felt Him near me and lovingly involved in my life. The one thing I never actually did was release complete control of my life to God.

By the time I was eighteen, I was a first year student at UCSB, living in the dorms with an ambitious attitude and an optimistic outlook. Like other first year students, I saw college as an adventure, a new beginning, and I was excited to make the most out of my experience. I quickly made friends with great people, but I was hesitant to get wrapped up in Isla Vista's party scene. Back in high school, I didn't view partying as a big deal. I kept my distance from the party scene until second quarter rolled around. By then I found myself progressively convinced that it was an acceptable way to let loose, forget about school, and have fun with my friends.

At this time, I still identified myself as a Christian. But I had grown distant from God and often avoided bringing my issues directly to Him. I used to feel a tug on my heart whenever I thought about God or occasionally mustered up the courage to be honest with Him. I knew God desired more for my life, but I convinced myself it would be useless to pursue a real relationship with Him while at UCSB.

On one particular Saturday night, I found myself walking down Del Playa with a friend, heading back to our dorms. We struck up a conversation with a random guy named Kyle hanging out in the road. After briefly chatting, Kyle told us he lived at the Jesus Burgers house. At this time I hadn't actually visited the Jesus Burgers house, but I had heard the people who lived there were pretty cool and generous. These people had a solid reputation for being friendly, feeding hundreds of people, and offering up their bathrooms every week, asking nothing in return.

Kyle politely asked us if we would be open to receive prayer from his friends at his house. Although we were a couple blocks away from the house and didn't really know what to expect, we were both open to it and followed him. We walked with him up the stairs of the Jesus Burgers house into a living room with about ten people (all about my age) hanging out with welcoming smiles on their faces. I felt completely at peace when I walked in the room. As I looked into the people's friendly eyes, I knew there was something greatly different about them. I sat down with my friend, and they began to pray for us.

I was shocked to hear the raw love of God flowing out of their mouths that spoke directly to my heart. As one girl prayed for each of us, she drew upon exact details about each of our lives that we had never mentioned to anyone. She knew personal details about me that no one could have known other than God Himself. She brought up my painful past and told me how God has loved and cared for me all my life, and that He desired an intimate relationship with me. The other girl shared that "God cares about the heaviness your heart has been experiencing and the void you are trying to fill. He wants to set you free from the pain of your past that you are carrying and give you life abundantly."

I tried to hold back my tears, but I was overwhelmed by the unadulterated truth these people were speaking to my heart. I cried, knowing that God was saying these things directly to me through these people. And I knew they could absolutely hear God. This confounded all that I had previously known concerning the limits of a relationship with God. In our day and age, I didn't know people could accurately interpret God's thoughts or feelings. I saved the number of one of the girls who prayed for me and thanked all of them. My friend and I walked home, trying to make sense of what just happened at the Jesus Burgers house.

I thought about that night over and over again.

But even after that night, I convinced myself that while in college I could never make the commitment that these people had made to God. Even though I knew God deeply cared about me and desired a loving relationship with me, I continually made excuses to myself that I didn't have the strength or ability to turn my life around and commit to that relationship. A year passed, and I continually distracted myself with good grades, friends, and partying. I desperately wanted to keep myself preoccupied to avoid facing the reality that I felt empty and was unhappy with my life.

Then I finally hit a dead end and began to face reality. Immersing myself into goals and aspirations no longer had the allure it once did to distract me from my life's meaninglessness. I felt alone even though I had people surrounding me all the time. My family and most of my friends assumed I was fine since they knew me as that strong girl who always had it together. But after months of feeling the emptiness, the pain of my past weighed on my chest, and I fell into depression. I used to wake up with terrible anxiety, feeling alone and worthless. My roommate at the time knew the extent of how bad my depression was, but I tried to hide it from everyone else.

One Sunday, my brother asked me to go to church with him, and I reluctantly went. When I walked into Isla Vista Church, I immediately had this peaceful, nostalgic feeling—I knew the presence of God was there. I sat in a pew listening to the amazing worship music and was brought to tears just by being in the presence of God. My heart pained and yearned, admitting and believing that a true relationship with God was what I needed to feel whole. All of a sudden, one of the girls who had prayed over me at the Jesus Burgers house over a year ago came up to me. She remembered who I was and asked if she could pray for me again. I agreed, and she began to talk about the desires in my heart to have freedom from the weight that I was carrying. She went on to say, "God desires to fill your heart with a love so strong that it will heal and renew you from the inside out."

As she prayed, I felt the unbearable pain surface in my chest. I broke down and cried out to God, knowing that I couldn't do this alone anymore. I felt helpless, and I fully knew that God was love and I needed Him in my life to live with purpose and fulfillment. I completely gave control of my life to God that day, knowing in my heart that He was the only way and my only hope. I finally trusted Him, took His hand, and walked away from my old self and never looked back. Thankfully, after I gave up control to God, I didn't have to focus on giving up my bad habits. I just set my sights on Jesus, and my bad habits burned off from the power of God's love pouring into my life, sealing up my cracks. Fully committing and giving my life to God was the best decision I have ever made; it shifted my life for the better in every aspect of my being.

I am now living a life entirely defined by love. I am eternally grateful that God never gave up on me and that He loved me unconditionally, even when I rejected and ignored Him. I have a sense of fulfillment now that I never could have attained on my own, despite all my efforts. The family of people that God has surrounded me with has selflessly loved and cared for me throughout my journey as well. The girl who prayed for me is now a good friend, and most of my close friends ended up falling in love with God shortly after I did. God also healed the relationships within my family, renewing all of our hearts for each other as a direct result of pursuing a relationship with Him. My friends and family never stop talking about how thankful we are for God in our lives, and they marvel at how He chose to love us first.

You will often find me at Jesus Burgers, Upper Room, or Isla Vista Church now, hanging out with my friends and enjoying life and true happiness. I guess you could say things in my life have come full circle since I now often pray for others and share what God's heart is for them. I have had the opportunity to return the favor to different people and see lives changed by God. The people involved with the Jesus Burgers ministry are phenomenal individuals who transform lives and spread the love of God on a daily basis. Now my friends and I, too, are passionate about sharing the love we have found in Jesus with other people in Isla Vista who are searching for something greater in their lives. Where would we be if someone hadn't taken the time to share that love with us?

HIS FAME,
NOT MINE

TARRA RARICK

"Come on, Tarra!" the coach shouted, "Show me how bad you want to be on this team!" As I came around the track for our three-mile time trial, my legs were tired and heavy, but my heart was determined to accomplish what I had set out to do: make the UCSB Women's Cross Country team. I ran right behind the other girl for the first mile and a half, but in each consecutive lap I fell off pace, and my chance of finishing under the required time of 18:45 was fading fast.

Fear came over me as I began to doubt myself, and my mind went into self-destruct mode, "You should have eaten a better breakfast. You should have done more mileage this summer. You're not as fit as these girls." These thoughts consumed me, threatening to take over.

For the last two laps, the team members huddled around every turn of the track and cheered louder than a stadium of soccer fans, giving me a jolt of excitement that spurred me on to the end. With 100 meters left, I gave it all I had and crossed the line at 18:44, too out of breath to shout for victory but overwhelmed with happiness in my heart. I had made the team.

The first few weeks after that I believed that God had helped me make this team, but only by a second to let me know it was not going to be easy. It certainly was not easy.

As a new member of the team, I wanted my teammates to like me. Looking in the mirror, I felt I needed to drop several pounds to not only keep up during workouts but also to feel good enough standing next to their lean bodies. My reflection told me I had some flaws to fix, and I couldn't afford to waste time. I never considered myself funny or outgoing growing up, but to make a good impression I had to get everyone laughing, or so I thought. Just as I was determined to make the team, my next goal was to make a name for myself and rise up as the underdog that everyone adored and admired.

Unfortunately, this desire for their approval was a deep insecurity that manifested itself through lame jokes, unhealthy eating habits, partying, and a lot of tears. It didn't matter when I had a cool story to tell, because I tried so hard to impress the girls that my words were often rude, offensive, or just plain awkward. It didn't matter when I lost seven pounds in two weeks, because even if I had a good workout or a solid race, I still had an endless list of things to improve on. It didn't matter when I would drink in the off-season to reveal my wild and "fun" side, because after showing up in my cutest outfit, dancing on the tables, and winning beer pong, I would always stumble back to my dorm knowing in my heart that I left no more accepted than when I arrived.

As weeks went by, I got to know the girls better and did my best to love them. Soon I could run with the pack and was only seconds behind some of them in races. Even my classes were going great. Everything seemed good, but I still went to bed many nights crying, unable to stop comparing myself to each girl and wondering what else I could fix and how I did so many things wrong. I pleaded for God to give me the strength to skip dessert, to make me witty, and yet to help me be myself because the person I was acting like wasn't really me. I wasn't sure if God would really answer those prayers, but I was desperate for someone to tell me I was doing a good job.

Throughout the quarter, I attended a Bible study, and every week I divulged my restless heart to these girls. One of the leaders always had a simple answer that encouraged me to rely on God. "Just keep praying about it" was what I heard, and with the tiniest bit of faith, I did. I prayed as often as I could remember, sincerely longing for an answer.

Winter break finally arrived, and I continued my high-mileage training as usual. A small rainstorm had blown through a couple nights before, so I decided to run along the green trails behind my parents' house. As I got closer, I felt overwhelmed by the beauty of the hills. Having a deep connection with nature, it struck me that this was the first time in months I had given my surroundings any thought; I had been so focused on running fast that everything else faded away. Suddenly I got a sharp side cramp, so I stopped to walk it out, taking a few moments to admire the splendor around me. I thought about the cross-country team. Within seconds my eyes overflowed with tears, and I began to sob uncontrollably, releasing all my sadness and confusion. I called out to God, telling Him everything I felt, and fell to my knees begging for help. "I don't know what to do!" I cried, "I love you, God! I just want what you want."

I heard God's voice more clearly that day than ever before. Cross-country running demanded all of me, but God wanted all of me. He told me He wasn't willing to take the back seat in my life anymore because He loved me too much. So I decided to quit. I was overcome with peace, but doubts quickly crept in. The thought of quitting felt so right, but my mind was whispering defeat, failure, and regret. To quit the team would mean throwing away seven years of training, to leave a NCAA conference championship team, and to give up becoming a legend. However, I felt unbelievably confident about my choice and didn't succumb to fear. Whenever I started to worry about what people would think, I remembered my run and trusted that God had a good plan for me. I didn't know what that plan was, but it was worth the risk.

After quitting, I felt free and invigorated! Before I knew it, I became immersed in fellowship in a campus Christian group, soaking up every drop of community like a sponge and going to every event, prayer meeting, and Bible study I could. Without my usual twelve-mile run on Sundays, I finally had time to go to church and see what it meant to be a part of the body of Christ. I was regularly attending a morning service at a church out of town, but every week my Bible study leader invited me to Isla Vista Church down the street. I finally decided to go, and I felt their love so tangibly that it almost seemed too good to be true. But it was real, and at the family dinners after the gathering I realized that this is how life is meant to be: loving others by receiving God's love first.

No longer was it about making a name for myself or becoming a legend in track. There was a far greater purpose He had created me for—making His name famous. My mind-set was completely transformed. The thought of receiving honor for myself was strange and uncomfortable, and I wanted nothing to do with it. Leaving my mark on history was all about me, but having an impact on eternity for His glory and honor was my new desire. Jesus Burgers soon became a place for me to live out this purpose.

As I started spending more time with God, my understanding of His character and His purpose for the world became clearer. Prayer became meaningful, the Bible became exciting, and the Holy Spirit became my best friend. This incredible joy was too good to keep to myself. I wanted to scream out to Del Playa how much God loves them, that it's not too late, and that they don't have to be ashamed of anything because Jesus forgives them. My heart began to break for Isla Vista like never before. As I prayed for the city, whole countries started popping up in my mind. Ethiopia, Thailand, the Philippines—places I had never once given a second thought to, I was now weeping over. Within weeks of forsaking my fame for God's, He was changing my perspective from saving one city to the entire world. At any moment I was willing to drop everything and buy a plane ticket to Africa to go make disciples, but God soon revealed to me the plans he had for Isla Vista to be an international home. The nations will come to us, and they will bring Love back to their country.

Through Jesus Burgers, God showed me that the nations are standing in our own front yard—literally! International students from all over the world come to this city to study at UCSB or to experience the party scene that it is so famously known for. The Jesus Burgers house happens to be the safe haven for people new to the raging city, so it is not uncommon for international students to show up on Friday nights.

One night at Jesus Burgers, as I was prepping the burger buns with ketchup and mustard, a kind-looking Japanese couple waited in line for their burgers. After they ate, they went inside the house to rest on the couch. I happened to be in there when they walked in, so I offered them water and struck up a conversation. Although they spoke very limited English, I shared a bit about myself and asked if they knew God or had any religion. To my surprise, they told me they had never heard of Jesus and didn't know the Bible. One didn't believe in God and the other prayed to Buddha.

I joyfully explained the Gospel to them as simply as possible. They listened intently, nodding as they understood. I asked if what I was explaining sounded good, and they both gave me an enthusiastic, "Yes!" Then I asked if they wanted Jesus to be in their hearts, and though the man hesitantly shook his head, he asked if we could go through the Bible together. We all exchanged numbers and are continuing to learn about God's love together. That night, they left knowing there was hope for eternal life.

Right after that conversation, I went to sit by the fire pit. A bleach blonde boy sat a couple seats away from me. I asked how his night was going and immediately heard his accent—he said he was from Holland. After a couple minutes of talking, another young man sat in the seat between us and joined in on our conversation. Another accent? This guy was from Britain. We shared stories, laughed, and started talking about their weed-smoking habits. I proceeded to tell them that the Holy Spirit was much better and a high beyond anything they could imagine. With a look of disbelief on their faces, I asked if they wanted to feel His presence, and they openly agreed. "Put out your hands and say, 'Holy Spirit come,' " I said, and they did exactly so. "Do you feel any tingling or warmth?" I asked, and my Dutch friend gasped and looked at me with eyes wide open, handed me his phone and told me to write down everything I just said to him. My British buddy cautiously examined his hands and proposed it could have been the fire pit. I had him stand back and ask again. "I definitely feel it," he smiled.

I began sharing my testimony and all of the ways God has changed my life. They were hanging on my every word, amazed by my authentic joy and in awe of what they had just experienced. These men left thankful, blessed, and touched by the love of God.

Jesus Burgers is a vessel of love. People from all over the world come and see this love heal their bodies, bind up their broken hearts, and give them faith that God is a good Father. Before I knew how much God loved me, my identity was based on the name I made for myself. Jesus proved to me that He is worth giving everything up for, and now I'm determined to make HIS name famous in all the earth.

BEAUTY FOR ASHES

CASSIE AROYAN

Imet Jesus through a friend during the early years of high school but quickly decided that a boyfriend was more important. It's wild to think that I saw a relationship that centered on jealousy, sex, and drugs more satisfying than the moments of noticeable freedom I had experienced with Jesus. When leaving for college, without a boyfriend or any relationship with God, I remember turning to take one last look at my room. I was checking to see if I had forgotten anything significant that I would need. I noticed my Bible on my nightstand and thought, I won't need that while I'm gone. I had absolutely no intention of rekindling my relationship with God and was fully aware of it. I also had no idea that Jesus had me in mind while I was on my way to an outrageous party school where I was trying to lose myself in the midst of sex, drugs, and alcohol.

It didn't take long for His plan to catch up with me: I got invited to attend a Christian club on campus called Real Life. I went because I didn't have anything else to do that night, and my best friend, Heather, wanted to check it out too. As I started going to the different events Real Life held, I met the most amazing people, some of whom are now best friends of mine. However, even amidst the newfound friendships and community I was discovering among Christian friends, my first year at college ended up being the balancing act of a scandalous, mischievous double life.

This all took place while I was barely trying to hold on to any possible relationship with God. I couldn't fathom letting go of my life in the world because I was hungry for relationship and an experience, and I didn't know yet that I could have this with God. I went through constant emotions of feeling isolated, depressed, guilty, and shameful, all the while lying to Christian friends about why I couldn't go to church events or hang out with Christian youth. Ironically, the only genuine love and care came from friends I had met who were Christian, yet they still weren't my first choice to spend time with on a Friday night, because I was so desperate for an experience. But ultimately, the double life wasn't working out for me.

The first supernatural encounter I had ever witnessed came during the first time I attended Isla Vista Church in the cozy backyard of the Lomelinos' home at the end of 2009. The power of the Holy Spirit fell upon us as Heather's back got healed because her legs grew out to equal lengths. I was in awe, of course, but it wasn't enough to change me. Even with this miracle, I wasn't willing to let go of the life I had found in the oh-so-familiar culture of Isla Vista. The parties, attention, sexuality, and carelessness of Isla Vista drew me in like it does so many other people. I found that the nights when I got drunk gave me stories to tell my friends—attention-grabbing experiences of regret or humor, which usually happened at the cost of someone else. Stories like these falsely made me believe I was doing something with my life.

In my first year of college, a friend of mine had been serving at Jesus Burgers on Friday nights, but my Friday nights were too valuable to me to sacrifice. It was my time to let loose, to feel some sort of value, and to experience anything the night had for me. I recall having a feeling of great expectancy of some sort of emotional experience each night of the weekend when I left my room. This outlook isn't uncommon in Isla Vista because something is always happening. When alcohol, drugs, and college kids are involved, you're bound to walk away with some sort of encounter or story. I would avoid walking by Jesus Burgers in the event that I might see someone who would recognize me and cause me to feel convicted or judged. I wanted nothing to do with conviction because I knew how real it was and how often it would ruin my nights.

A Friday night had finally come around during which I didn't feel like partying, and some friends spent some time convincing me to go to the Upper Room and Jesus Burgers. I went, fearful of feeling rejected and judged, but my experience was absolutely the opposite. Let me just tell you, Holy Spirit loves Upper Room. His children get to come with whatever they choose to carry, yet He continuously is generous and explosive. I remember watching people cry as a result of encountering God's love. I asked Him why I never got emotionally affected when I came to Him, like crying out of joy or His overwhelming love. I wanted an encounter and felt like I had never experienced the power of God. I had felt numb to His presence for quite some time, and then all of a sudden, in a shed behind a house on a crazy party street, I started weeping uncontrollably. My friend asked why I was crying, and I responded something like, "I don't know, but I think it's the love of God." He chose to reveal Himself in the safest setting around the safest people. I asked Him for an experience, and He gave me one! All we have to do is ask!

Summer was approaching. Realizing I didn't have plans, I decided to go on a mission trip. Deep down it was not because I wanted to share the love of Christ with others, but because I really liked Hawai'i and was reluctant to spend a whole summer back at home.

My relationship with God felt nowhere near whole as my mission trip grew closer. It was so far away, in fact, that I drove out to Santa Cruz the week before leaving to see the same boyfriend that drew me away from God before college. I'm not sure what my initial intentions were, but they weren't anywhere near pure, and I ended up having sex with him. Looking back, I know I was definitely convicted, but my relationship with God was too shallow to bring healing and restoration; so I was left with guilt and shame.

As I got settled in Hawai'i with my belongings, along with all of the shame, guilt, and confusion I was carrying, my roommate, Jasmine, established a realness that communicated to me I was free to lay down the heavy emotions I was carrying. She encouraged me to face the Father rather than hide behind time spent with friends or even trying to do work for God. He is much more interested in relationship with us than the works we can do for Him.

During the first two weeks, God poured out so much of His presence, grace, and love on me that I was completely transformed. I had tears of joy rather than pain—and a hunger that I knew would never cease. After He lifted my burdens, restored my heart, and destroyed my walls, I felt in union with Him once again. As if that wasn't enough, I radically encountered the love of God firsthand at a Holy Spirit retreat I attended with great expectation. My friend received the gift of tongues. As I tried to interpret, I was brought to tears. He spoke directly to me, saying that I was worth the price of death, and of all of the times that I had ever walked away or chosen some-one over Him, He never left me. He took me from my ashes to beauty all because He loves me. God had unleashed His love in a way that made me commit to never hardening my heart again at the sound of His voice.

My favorite nights at Jesus Burgers are those that involve drunk college kids with no hope of getting home for the night. I love when we offer rides, but many don't know how to accept them, even though it is not anywhere near a burden to offer a ride in the first place. Even though they are sick to their stomach with their head in a bag the whole drive—whether the destination is their own home, a friend's house, or the hospital—I know that Jesus has enough love for them all. My favorite time to serve someone is when I know that there isn't anything they can do in return. Usually I never again see the people I drive home. I know that if someone were to have crossed Jesus' path who needed a lift somewhere, He would have dropped everything.

There is so much joy in serving drunken college students on a Friday night. A ride isn't a burden, be-cause we aren't burdens to Him. Half of the people don't know how to say thank you; half of them think we're angels. It's one of my favorite ways to love the weekend warriors of IV.

My heart has been broken by God for this city, and I want to be willing to provide the people of Isla Vista an opportunity to encounter the love of God, because that is how He so radically revealed Himself to me. I was hungry for an experience and, of course,

He provided one. That's what I was seeking in the beginning of my endeavors in Isla Vista and even in high school. I believe so many people are looking for the same thing. That's where we come in. "We love Him because He first loved us," (1 John 4:19) and then we pour out His love on others.

HE'S ALWAYS FAITHFUL

HEATHER TUPPS

I grew up in what many would call a tradition-
al Christian home—one in which we attended
church every week—and I gave my life to Jesus in
the fourth grade. While I fully understood the truth
in my decision, I didn't know what a commitment to
Jesus looked like because I didn't know anyone who
had an actual relationship with God. Until my junior
year of high school, life consisted of moving all over
the country and experiencing a variety of Christian
cultures in Delaware, Pennsylvania, Ohio, Florida,
and Northern California. My definition of a relationship with God changed and morphed into what was
socially acceptable in each town I moved to. For ex-
ample, in Ohio, being a Christian consisted of going
to church on Sundays, being a dedicated Ohio State
football fan, and of course, partying because "there's
nothing else to do in this town."

Halfway through high school, I moved to
Northern California and tried to have a relationship
with God by attending youth group, going on mission trips, and dating the high school worship leader.
In retrospect, I had only given half of my heart to

Jesus, resisting complete transformation. The void in my heart was very present as I began to compromise my relationship with God to prioritize what I deemed more important: my relationship with my boyfriend. We ended up pulling each other further away from the Lord as we both lived in denial of our sin. I clearly recognized the conviction of the Holy Spirit, but ignored His promptings. It wasn't until I moved to Santa Barbara that I began to understand what a real, unique relationship with Jesus Christ actually was.

I moved to Isla Vista in 2009 with my best friend Cassie for school. We both expressed a desire to find a church, but for the first month that desire was replaced with a stronger urge to fit in and have fun. Thankfully, the partying didn't last long, and I quickly got plugged in with a Christian club on campus. After a few weeks of attending the weekly meetings, I was reminded of God's mercy and the steadfast love I knew as a child. I repented for being so openly disobedient and truly gave all of my heart to Him.

In November of 2009, I came to Isla Vista Church for the first time and got wrecked by the Holy Spirit. I honestly can't tell you how I ended up in the Lomelinos' backyard that fall night, huddled in blankets and surrounded by new friends. It must have been the Holy Spirit that led me there.

Around that time, I had to see a chiropractor regularly to deal with some spinal problems, and that whole evening I was frustrated with my back pain. Someone went up to the front of the church and asked if anyone was having lower back pain. Without thinking, my hand shot up, and he asked if he could pray for it to be healed. I had zero faith that anything would happen, but I agreed to let him pray. As I was sitting, he held up my legs to show that one was about half an inch shorter than the other. He confidently said he was going to pray for it to grow out, explaining that the God of the New Testament is still living and active, wanting to completely heal us of every sickness and affliction. I will never forget the wide eyes and dropped jaw of Cassie standing in front of me exclaiming "Heather . . . your leg is growing right now!" as he prayed for my leg. Immediately, all the pain was gone, and I haven't gone to a chiropractor since.

That first encounter jump-started a hunger for a relationship with the living God that was accompanied by the gifts of the Spirit. The realization that He not only heals and speaks to us but also wants us to have a life of adventure makes a relationship with God so much more exciting! It gives a new meaning to the Bible being the living word of God. I could no longer go days without thinking of Him because His love was suddenly so relevant, so tangible. As I gave Him room to move, He never failed to show up.

By spring of my freshman year, I had become fairly involved in Isla Vista Church and the Jesus Burger ministry, and I was planning on living with three of my Christian friends there the following year. But of course, God knows me better than I know myself and had other plans for me. The girls in my suite kept asking if I would live with them in a house of ten girls who all lived the party lifestyle. I would just laugh whenever they mentioned it because that sounded like the worst possible living situation ever. One day I was on a run and just started weeping with love for the girls in that house because none of them knew Jesus. God clearly spoke to me and told me that I needed to live there. After receiving His heart for them, how could I say no? Later that week, the three friends that I wanted to live with called me saying there were only three spots next door to the Jesus Burgers house and that they were moving in. I'll admit their excitement made me really mad at God. I cried for about a week worrying about the terror that lay ahead and thinking that I had been hustled by God.

The next year was, as I expected, crazy. On several nights I would wake up three or four times from parties and music. One night I even called the cops on my own house for a noise complaint! It was a year filled with tears and the ever persistent question, "Why me God?" But I was so blessed to have members of the church always encouraging me to stay strong.

Aly, whom I had roomed with before, let me pray for her and talked with me about Jesus, but respectfully held on to her atheist views. I became close friends with Rasta, a girl from Orange County who was really hungry for an experience with God. She came to church with me a few times and got wrecked by the love of God through some very accurate and detailed prophetic words. She couldn't believe that God knew she loved to write and play piano. She was so touched that she drove home and got one of the other roommates to come and hear what God knows about her. Both of them encountered God with tears, laughter, and hugs. Unfortunately, they weren't ready to dive in and give up the Isla Vista lifestyle, but I knew that God had met them in a real way.

There were some nights that Jesus told me to stay home and go to the parties my housemates were throwing rather than go to Jesus Burgers. Many Christians were concerned about whether or not I was hearing God correctly, forgetting that most of Jesus' miracles were performed outside the walls of the church while He was with sinners and prostitutes. If Jesus could live amongst them and remain holy and perfect, then why can't His daughter, created in His image, containing the fullness of God, do the same? Those nights were miraculous—surrounded by girls in short skirts and high heels, I would chill in my jeans and sweatshirt. Party guests would come up to me wondering why I wasn't drinking or dressed up. My availability and their curiosity allowed me to prophesy over them about what God sees in them and how much He knows and loves them. One time I prophesied over a girl about how she loved God in high school and has been missing the feelings that she had during that time. She broke down crying on my shoulder next to the beer pong table while people watched, very confused. She told me about how she used to go on Mexico mission trips and that she thought about those times often. After recognizing how much God was still pursuing her, she began to share the love of God with the beer pong crew. It was a sight to see!

In another instance, I got into a spiritual conversation with a guy and told him why I believe in Jesus. I felt led to ask about his life, his dad, and his abandonment issues. He began crying and told me that his father committed suicide the year before after a fight they had. That one word from God completely opened his heart as he began telling me things that he has never told anyone, including certain encounters that he had that made it impossible to deny the existence of Jesus. Jesus loves to show up amongst these broken people and reveal His love to them, because they're His children. His love pursues them passionately and faithfully, even when they openly hate Him for the pain of their pasts. I mean c'mon, that's a good Father!

I'm so thankful for the Jesus Burgers ministry that has equipped and encouraged me to do what I felt like Jesus was saying, even if it seemed completely irrational. Toward the end of the year, I became friends with one of my housemates' twin named Cori and invited her to church and Campus Crusade. We started going together and she loved it. But as the year came to an end, it seemed to me that the fruit God promised with my housemates was not going to happen.

The next year, I moved into the Jesus Burger house, Aly moved to San Francisco, and Rasta moved home to Orange County. I happened to have a class with Cori and her twin, Kristin, in the fall and found out that they had been attending church consistently that summer while I was away doing ministry in Kansas City. I eventually got to see them dedicate their lives to Jesus that quarter, and they both asked me to disciple them! The relationships that I still have with them have been the greatest blessings. Not only are they now radical lovers of Jesus, they still live with the same girls that I lived with last year. Cori and Kristin are leading the outreach team next year through Campus Crusade, which will undoubtedly have a great influence on the community. While Cori is very committed to Campus Crusade and will be living at their community house next year, Kristin will be living in the Jesus Burgers home with me. To my absolute enjoyment, they have taken my place and are now the ones bringing the housemates to church and Jesus Burgers. This year we are contending together to see that house completely transformed by the love of God. Furthermore, Aly, who was an atheist for the two years I lived with her, became a Christian in San Francisco this year and is really involved with a church and Campus Crusade there!

I now cringe when I think of that pitiful question, "Why me God?" Although I couldn't see it at the time, He is always faithful. He knows what we can handle, and I am so thankful to have been able to experience the reward of seeing three girls come to Christ. It was well worth the frustration and pain. He indeed has plans to prosper us and not to harm us, bringing us a bright future.

GIVE YOUR PAIN TO JESUS

CHRISTIAN SMITH

66 Can I make it up the stairs without being noticed?" The thought made my palms sweaty. My insides felt like an empty shell, dead to my past life, and drying up as I avoided any interactions with my previous Christianity. I awkwardly slid out of my girlfriend's car, keeping my back turned toward the neighbors. Taking the stairs two by two, I reached the top and quickly jumped through the door. The whole exercise of avoidance was exhausting.

I was nervous about the idea of facing my past on a daily basis. Just two years before, the house I was avoiding was my home; the people I didn't want to interact with previously were my friends. I had embraced everything I now avoided. Now, I was living part time with my girlfriend, who happened to live next door to the Jesus Burgers house. The irony glared back as I looked out the window at my old house and pondered the path that brought me into the present moment.

Three years before, Santa Barbara had welcomed me on the drive in with a full moon bathing the ocean in light on a late summer evening. I was attending the

University of California, Santa Barbara, as a freshman and very excited to learn and grow on my own. I grew up in a Christian home and fostered a deep connection with God in the early years of my life during powerful encounters with the presence of God. I learned to hear God's voice at a young age and was often able to understand what was going on in a person's life without prior knowledge. Throughout high school, I maintained a connection with God and was able to stay set apart from indulging in vices my peers would chase.

Now that I was starting college, a whole new atmosphere of choices and responsibilities opened up to me. I was fortunate to forge a strong relationship with a Christian friend early in my college career, and we looked around at various options to get plugged into a church. We landed at Isla Vista Church, a young, radical group of people who were passionate to see God move in the city. I felt like I fit right in with the family. Throughout the first year of school, I was able to create a strong community around me and grow with God.

My first experience with Jesus Burgers was one I'll never forget. The first week of school was wrapping up, and my friend Reis and I bundled up for our journey into Isla Vista. As we skated from the dorms into IV, the spiritual atmosphere all around us seemed so dark. IV seemed like a scary place. There were throngs of thoroughly inebriated party people yelling obscenities on poorly lit streets littered with broken glass. Reis and I jumped right into helping manufacture and hand out the coveted Jesus Burgers to all the neighbors out and about. I didn't know what to say to people, so I let others do the talking. I began to see people powerfully encounter God, and it made me excited and bold to see others know God. I made the commitment to live in the Jesus Burgers house my second year of school.

I had stellar grades and felt close to God. All was going well until I heard the news that my mother was becoming very ill. My mother had been diagnosed with breast cancer when I was a freshman in high school. Years of prayer, ministry trips, changes in diet, and other treatment had sent the cancer into remission. Both my parents and I held on to faith that Jesus was going to heal Mom. There was no doubt in my mind that God was going to intervene and heal her. I held on to hope.

The week before finals, I received a voicemail from my father. "Christian, your mother is not doing well," his voice, strong and calm, was reassuring. "Things are progressing quickly. We don't know how much longer Mom will be with us. You need to come home."

My body plunged into my sick stomach, dunking my entire body into the nausea. I was in a state of disbelief and didn't know what to do. I drove home on adrenalin and muscle memory. When I arrived home, Mom was sitting in her armchair, pale. Her eyes were sunk into her head. I grabbed her hand; she still had strength. Her smile beamed. We talked and sat together for hours, savoring every moment. The clock ticked through to late Sunday afternoon, and our time together was winding down because I had to go back to IV to take three finals. "Christian," my mom whispered, the strength in her words coming from a place of peace, "our bodies are shells and our spirits live on. When I go on, remember, give your pain to Jesus." I held her and cried into her shoulder.

After the onslaught of finals, I stayed up all night, packing my dorm room. I left as quickly as I could and drove home with my stomach full of tangled knots. I arrived home to a house full of mourning. My five-year-old brother ran out and grabbed my shirt to get my attention. "Christian, Christian, Mom is dead." There wasn't an ounce of understanding in his innocence. He didn't know what he just said. My heart broke as I stumbled into the house to the bed where Mom lay.

"God, raise her back to life! I know you can do it." I prayed for hours in the room, but to no avail. Nothing in the room moved. I was in disbelief. "God, how could you do this?" A small fissure was introduced into my relationship with God.

Blow by blow, my life transformed over the next sixteen months into something I never imagined it would become. The cracks in my life began to show as the stress increased. My life as I knew it began to fall apart. I struggled to maintain righteousness, and I became prone to depression. I was not able to connect who I thought God to be and what I now experienced.

As my pursuit of a technical degree continued into my second year, the amount of time I spent with God waned. I struggled to stay connected with God as my schedule became progressively busier with difficult classes and time-consuming projects. Mental and spiritual distractions began to surface. I moved further and further away from church. I couldn't do anything to wipe away the pain and depression.

I reached the breaking point. "God, I can't see the God I knew when I was young," I prayed. "God, I'm going to repent of what I believe about You. I am going to repent from believing in You at all." I wiped the slate clean. I stopped going to church because it wasn't helping me. I stopped talking to my friends because they didn't bring me peace, insight, or answers. I started living and doing what was right by me.

Two years later, my life came full circle: I was living

with my girlfriend, in denial of my past and who God was. But it all had to end. I was unsatisfied with what the world had to offer. I had a series of out-of-body experiences in which God reached into my life and called my name. In those experiences, the voice of God and the spiritual realm became real again. Jesus asked me if I knew the day and the hour I was living in. He showed me how terrifying life would be without His presence. The difference between light and darkness became stark and in my face. When I realized God loved me just the way I was in that moment, I began to walk back with Jesus. As I gave Him the pain and guilt I felt, He healed me and gave me peace. God was able to defeat and heal the heartache of my mother's death and renew my hope for an abundant life. After that, it did not take long for God's love to bring me back into the Isla Vista Church family and to find myself serving at Jesus Burgers from time to time. The house I had once tried to avoid was again a reminder of the love and goodness of God, even through the trials of life.

Today I know God is real and His love supersedes any situation that can arise. Jesus was faithful to chase me down and bring me back into the Father's love. He created us; He knows every sinew holding together every muscle, wrapped around every bone, and He fashioned it all out of the dust of the earth. If He can make us out of dust, what unimaginable glory can He make out of our pain? I finally made a decision to follow my mom's advice and give Him my pain, and I haven't looked back since.

WITH HIM

LINDSAY SLAVIK

Like many, I grew up around the church. I say around because I did not really feel like I was in the church. I participated in all the church events: Sunday school, retreats, Bible studies, and mission trips, but nothing ever felt real in my heart. None of my leaders had solid answers to my many questions about God; all I learned was that I could live *for* God by my involvement at these church events. What I did not learn was that I could live *with* God. Living for him and not with Him was lifeless. God is life Himself, beyond any church program or Sunday school lesson. I eventually got bored with church and excited by the many pleasures of the world.

By the time I began high school, I had decided to stop attending church because I got too busy. My life consisted of competition dancing, working hard for good grades, partying, and consistently dating different guys. My dance career eclipsed all other aspects of my life. I was completely obsessed with my technique, achievements, and career as a pre-professional dancer.

Every summer throughout high school, I lived in

New York to train with professional ballet and modern dance companies. I did everything I could to steward this passion of mine. However, I took it to an extreme. A few subtle critiques about my physique, along with my dancing in front of a mirror all day, created a distorted mind-set that consumed me. These thoughts turned into actions, spiraling out of control in the form of an eating disorder. Consequently, I starved myself because I thought I was improving myself and my dance technique by eating less.

My world and my attempt to control it came crashing down on me at the end of high school. My identity as a competition dancer and all the things I had strived for—appearance, grades, reputation—did not mean anything anymore because a new chapter of life was about to begin: college. I realized that dance, like every other thing in my life, was not completely satisfying, and I hated being stuck in this lifestyle of trying to control every part of my life. It was slowly killing my soul.

That summer I began going to church again with my older sister. The worship lyrics on the screen blurred together like a bunch of fluffy words that had no meaning. On our way back home, I would cry because I knew there had to be something more to those worship songs, but I did not know how to connect with them.

Soon after that I was on my way to college at the University of California, Santa Barbara. As a dancer, all I wanted was to be in New York or Los Angeles, but I unhappily settled for UCSB. I planned on transferring as soon as possible, but God had other plans. He was the one who orchestrated my college destination, and He had His own plans to radically change my heart, my mind, and my life!

It all began with one simple song. I was invited to

go to a retreat for Real Life. On the first night my eyes were opened. During worship, I was reading the lyrics on the screen once again; but this time, suddenly I understood them! Truth just hit me out of nowhere; God is real and He really loves me. His Son really did die so that I could live eternally with God, no longer just for Him. I began crying. I was overwhelmed by these truths coming to life; God was real, this was all real! From that night on, my life forever changed, and I became consumed with the desire to know God and all of His mysterious glory.

I woke up early that next week, pulled out my journal, and started writing to God. All those same questions I had asked my church leaders years ago came pouring out of my pen, but this time I decided to go straight to the source. Later that night I met up with some of the girls from Real Life. We decided to go to Jesus Burgers. At that time I had no clue what Jesus Burgers was, but I knew I would be with people who loved God. So I was happy. I felt safe with them. I ended up in what I came to know as the prayer shed, where people were praying and worshiping before the outreach part of the night began. This whole experience in my new life with God had already felt like an exciting adventure, but little did I know it was about to get even crazier.

The prayer shed was filled with a varied assortment of people of all different ages, styles, and walks of life. They were all worshiping God in their own unique ways. Some were lying down, some were dancing, some were crying, some were hugging, and some were laughing. I sat down feeling a little uncomfortable, but also strangely excited.

I closed my eyes and started worshiping God. Suddenly, there was a hand on my head. A young Armenian woman was standing over me speaking in a language I had never heard before—a language that I came to know as tongues. She knelt down beside me with a huge smile and love in her eyes, and said, "Hi, I'm Meri. God loves you a lot!" with a laugh. Then she proceeded to answer every question that I had asked God that very morning. I started crying and laughing at the same time. I was so overwhelmed that God had heard my questions and that He loved me enough to speak through Meri to answer them.

Fast forward a year: I had become one of those crazy people I had first seen in the prayer shed. But now, they didn't seem so crazy. They were my family members, and they were crazy for God. The pastor, Jason, and his wife, Holly, took me under their wings as a spiritual daughter, and I learned how to hear God speak to me the same way Meri had heard God for me that fateful night. A group of us began going out from Jesus Burgers to find people on the street whom God highlighted to us; and we would go tell them what God was speaking to us about them. It was seriously the best time, the biggest high I could imagine—experiencing the love of God and then letting God use us to let others experience it too!

Soon after, I moved into the Jesus Burgers ministry house and continued to go out every Friday night with Jesus Burgers for the next three years. It was the most exciting night of my week. I loved loving people with Love Himself! We had so many incredible nights of people getting radically changed by encounters with God. We prayed for people, prophesied over people, and befriended people. We welcomed them in to use our bathroom or to hang out around the house. Whatever we did, people felt God's love through it all.

It was such a sweet time of my life. I grew so much through the community of family members I lived with and through the experiences I had out on the streets. I've learned that the reason this ministry functions so well is because of the culture of family and grace that Isla Vista Church has cultivated for years. When we come to know our sole identity as a child of God and a member of His Kingdom family, we are freed from our old selves and free to share His love with nothing holding us back!

There are so many stories to tell from those nights, but one in particular involves my dear friend Greg. Greg has been one of my best friends since we were twelve years old. We have seen each other through all of the rocky times that our teenage years brought us. By God's perfect plan, we ended up going to college together at UCSB.

Throughout college, Greg saw my life transform; he saw how I went from a starving, dance-obsessed girl to a new creation, a secure, beloved daughter of God. We would spend many hours discussing how God renewed my heart and my mind. He was always interested and excited about the thought of all of this being true, but he did not have hope that God could really change his own life. But I had faith for Greg, and when he finally hit rock bottom in his junior year of college, I was ready and expectant that God would move powerfully in his life. Greg had gotten to a point where he was drinking almost every day and was constantly high. Like my eating disorder and idolatry of dance, Greg was consumed by these counterfeits that were killing his soul, as well as his physical body.

One night at Jesus Burgers a prominent healing evangelist, Todd White, spoke at our worship gathering and did ministry with us on the streets. After worship, Todd and a few of us went out into the street to pray and prophesy over people. We were walking by a huge party, and I grabbed Todd because

I knew we were supposed to go in there. There were two bouncers blocking the entrance and a line of people trying to get in, making it nearly impossible for our crew to enter.

As we discussed the situation, Todd started walking toward the party. I turned around to see that the entrance was completely cleared; the bouncers and line of people were gone—so we all walked right on in. I knew my friend Greg was in there, and I also knew that God was longing to have His way with Greg's heart like He had with mine.

Moments later I spotted Greg dancing on a balcony. Somehow through the mob of party people, he spotted me, too. He came down in complete shock that I would even be at this party. I responded honestly that I came for him. All of a sudden, Todd was in his face pouring the love of God onto Greg; he started prophesying over Greg, telling Greg who he was and naming what he was struggling with and how God created him for something far greater.

I started crying as I saw God speak through Todd straight into Greg's heart! Anxiously, he struggled to leave my loving grasp and repeated, "I can't handle this, this is too much. I don't want to cry here." But I held on, repeating, "No Greg, it's okay, this is the love of God!" Finally he stopped fighting it and began crying and hugging me. He was instantly sobered as his eyes were opened to the power of God speaking through Todd White. Greg was overwhelmed—he was filled with so much joy because he had finally understood the truth in his heart. He had encountered the one true Almighty God—and nothing could compare!

Like I once had been, Greg was in bondage to the pleasures of the world and the schemes of the enemy that were out to steal, kill, and destroy us. But God had a plan to uniquely reach both of us in our lowest points and change us by His love! Greg, like me, is one of thousands of broken students who come to live in Isla Vista for college and each of whom God desires to encounter! We are His children, and we are created to live life in Him, renewed in His presence.

That is the sole purpose of the Jesus Burgers ministry: to live in our true identity as sons and daughters and bring others into the Kingdom family, restoring the relationship of the children of God with their loving Father.

AN
UNQUENCHABLE
FIRE

ANNALISA MORRIS

I remember being dragged to church as a young girl and always feeling bored and unfulfilled. But when I was in sixth grade my sister told me about a local youth group. This group was different. I felt cared for by the people and had a lot of fun at the youth events. On a small rafting trip with the group, I dedicated my life to Christ. I felt moved to tears for the first time (though not the last) by the sacrifice He made for me.

I knew that I was different from that day forward, yet it felt like the most natural thing at the same time. This God I barely knew seemed to give reason to the moral urges I had always felt. He gave a name to the One I called out to from fear in the night. This all led to a heartfelt but mediocre teenage faith that was filled with ups and downs, feeling Him and then not, rededications of faith followed by guilty slip-ups.

In college, I immediately got involved with a campus Christian group. I found some good friends there and a group of believers who were pursuing God authentically because they wanted to, not because anyone told them to. It was amazingly beautiful, though I had so much more to learn.

My connection with the Jesus Burgers ministry all started with a pack of water bottles. Nothing fancy, probably Arrowhead or Costco brand, but it turned my world upside down nonetheless. Some friends had bought a few packs of plastic water bottles and were going to hand them out to the partiers at Jesus Burgers; they asked if I wanted to come. "Jesus Burgers? What's that?" I retorted.

I found myself immersed in a crowd of people that I called my neighbors, but whom I had no real love for or connection with. The girls wore little clothing, the boys stood a little too close, and the alcohol they consumed never interested me. Their lifestyle was so different from mine, and one I held in disgust and contempt. As we traversed the party crowds that filled Del Playa, I began to question this thinking. Jesus called me to love my neighbors, right? He called me to live here, didn't He?

I met some Christians who were having conversations with some of the partygoers, and I saw how they were able to relate to these people, though the Christians were so different from the partiers.

Scared and nervous, I tried to start a conversation of my own. From these first interactions, I saw that these inhabitants of Isla Vista just wanted to be heard. The neighbors around me wanted to be cared for. I realized these people weren't that different from me at all. Everyone has a need to be loved and to belong. I didn't have to steer the conversation towards Jesus, because He would come up if He was supposed to. All I had to do was be available and share that same love God has given to me.

Sharing God's love felt amazing. I found purpose out in that yard; I found a heart of love for these people who could care less about Jesus. From the first night in that yard, gathered around the fire pit and grill, I was hooked.

Yet the real story for me was not in the front yard, but in the back. Tucked away behind the house where we did ministry was a place called the prayer shed: a two-car garage converted into a comfy, carpeted refuge where we would worship, pray, and encounter God before doing ministry. The thrown together, mismatched decor, the different paintings and half-finished murals, and the chalkboard with verses and drawings created this unique room that carried peace and an expectation for God to move.

This is the God we know and call upon: one who moves in power, and who cares enough to pursue the broken and go after those in darkness. It was in this place that I discovered the intimacy God created us for. It was in this room that I learned God could be much more than a faraway friend that I called upon in times of trouble. He was my husband, my best friend, my home, my purpose, my future, my everything.

I kept coming to Jesus Burgers, and I connected with many other Christians who were running the ministry, especially Jason Lomelino, the pastor of Isla Vista Church. One night, somewhat out of place, a man pulled up with a camera crew. He looked way too groomed and well dressed for Isla Vista, but his eyes shown with a light like I hadn't seen before. He said he was traveling all over, filming healing, prophecy, and God's work in the Kingdom for a TV show *Kingdom Reality*.

On a laptop, we watched videos of the man we just met praying for people and we saw God pouring out miraculous healing, signs, and wonders. We were shocked. We hadn't been exposed to this before. It was radical seeing how the Holy Spirit can move, almost to the point of scary and uncomfortable; really just unknown. My best friend, Lindsay, began to ask our pastor question after question as I sat in silence.

His answers were interrupted as the small living room began to fill with people and our TV friend came in.

Apparently, this man was somewhat well known in some Christian circles, and people wanted to have him pray for them. He asked if we had anyone in particular we wanted him to pray for; Jason nominated Lindsay and me.

The kind-hearted, soft-spoken man prayed for me and breathed destiny and purpose into the dry and lonely places. He began to tell me that I was called to unify people, to be a leader of nations. He spoke of places I would go and the visions I would fulfill in my life. He prophesied that I had been seeking my purpose and future and that God would speak to me about this. He would reveal it to me. He probably didn't know how right he was. This very question had filled my journal for the past few months, and God was opening the door to what my heart was longing for: real relationship.

In a moment, Lindsay's life and my life were changed as we cried together on a crowded living room floor.

The traveling prophet performed more miracles of healing and prophecy that night, but I already had been changed forever. There was nothing more that anyone could do for me. I discovered in that crowded living room at three in the morning that the God of all the universe not only knew me, but cared for me. He wanted to give me vision and see it fulfilled. He wanted to speak to me. He wanted to be my best friend and constant companion.

The journey didn't slow down from there; it only accelerated. As my eyes were opened to this new understanding of God, I was compelled to seek Him as I never had before. If He wanted to be my best friend I wasn't going to stop Him—I was going to invite

Him in and watch Him change me. As I continued on this journey and stayed involved with Jesus Burgers, I began to bring others along too. Other believers' eyes began to open to the intimacy we can experience with God, to His loving voice, and His incomparable Spirit. They would see that God wanted to speak to them, and that they too could experience the priesthood of all believers. In this discovery, there were many exclamations of, "Why has no one ever told me this?" I asked that very same question. So, I decided to start telling people.

In prayer and through hearing God's voice, I found myself. I didn't have to go on a road trip; I didn't have to recklessly get "fill-in-the-blank" out of my system. I didn't have to stray from friends, family, and everything I knew. I had to let go and let God show me who He is, and then, consequently, show me who I am. Through countless experiences, times of prayer and worship, God defined me, my value, my worth, my calling.

I had the privilege of living at the Jesus Burger house for two years of my college career. I learned so much during that time about what it meant to be in the family of God, how to live and love a community authentically, no matter the cost. I experienced the authority God places on us all, and what it was like to have a burden for a group of people and a location — and how to give that burden back to God. Breaking the bondage of insecurity and proving things to others, once finally severed, led me to freedom and to vulnerability with people and with God. I could be fully myself and release others to be fully themselves. We can all use our gifts, personalities, and dreams to further God's love and glory.

In this transformation, God birthed my dream for a prayer house: A place where people could experience the same intimacy that had defined me. A home where hearts could flourish and be released into the glory they were meant for before time began. God showed me that this would start a fire that could not be quenched—one we truly would not wish to quench.

One particular night we were hanging out around our living room, relaxing and cracking jokes, when a knock came on the door. It was a girl who we were somewhat familiar with from the community. She had a sling around her arm and came to our house asking for prayer and expecting God to heal her because she knew that was what we believed and that was what we would go after. We prayed, and she may or may not have felt better, but she felt loved. The point was she felt a need for love and for God, and she knew a place in Isla Vista that wanted to give that to her. God has provided a place for this to happen, and it came from the culture that Jesus Burgers created.

One year I was coordinating a week of 24-7 prayer before Halloween. A few of us would get together and change the setup of the room, vary the activities in there, get campus groups to sign up for time slots, and pray for God to move in the city. I was about to go down to the prayer shed to fulfill an hour I signed up for. I was thinking about my own heart for prayer. Slow, creeping thoughts started to condemn me. I knew I was seen as this prayer warrior, but I also knew how unfaithful I could be to pray for Isla Vista myself.

God spoke to me right then in my heart, "You are the catalyst. You are starting a fire that can't be stopped." I saw a vision of a flame going out from our small prayer shed and into all the nations. I thought about my friends and the ways they change people's lives: one transforming the dance community, another making friends with an Australian and seeing his life rocked by love, another sharing a simple prophetic word in a coffee shop that changed the course of a person's life. God showed me the ways that I've affected these friends' lives—the way I've loved them and set them free or supported them to be all God has said they would be. He said, "Their fruit is your fruit. The body shares the fruit."

But now that I think back, I really wasn't the catalyst. He was always the catalyst. Jesus Burgers, prayer, and the culture it created allowed me to experience intimacy and freedom. Jesus Burgers has started a fire that will affect our whole world—one burger at a time. Mark my words.

WATERING
SEEDS

BRAELYN MONTGOMERY

I always knew who God was, but I never knew who I was. For the longest time I thought that pleasing God meant to sacrifice everything good in life and become a miserable nobody with zero personality and independence. So, as exciting as that sounded, of course, I rebelled. If I couldn't live up to "God's standards" then I would live up to my own. And my standards consisted of being all that I could be for one boy.

Love in so many ways can be manipulated into whatever we think is good. I thought we had a good love, but in reality I was being mistreated sexually, emotionally, and spiritually. I drove myself to the ground with this boy. I even began to sacrifice all of my standards for his standards. That's what I thought love was: giving everything you've got whether or not you get anything in return. In a sense this statement is valid, but only in the purity of the Father's love for us. However, my relationship with this boy was the complete opposite of the Father's love. I do not mean to diminish or dishonor this man, but the truth is that there were so many lies in my heart that the enemy saw and used through him. The bottom line was that no one ever told me I was worthy to be loved or that my dreams and ideas mattered.

That all changed when I met Mac Montgomery. Mac and I met when he was stuck in religion, and I was stuck in depression. But God is good right? Although our hearts weren't in the perfect place and we weren't the perfect couple, Mac changed my life. And that was only because He always knew who the Father was, religious or not. It only took me a few years to realize that Mac had what I needed. I ran for so long from Mac, most likely because I wanted to run from God. But neither of them ever gave up. Mac knew what I was called to do and who I was supposed to be, and he wasn't satisfied to let me stay where I was. After my relentless effort to get him as far from me as possible, God broke me. I realized that God was for me, not against me. He was for my dreams and for my heart. And in this, I realized that was all Mac was trying to give me all along; he only wanted to open my eyes to see the truth of God's love, and to water the seeds of the goodness and beauty in me in order to see it grow.

That was how I first came to Isla Vista and became a part of this family. I maybe didn't know it at first, but I was always meant for family! My spirit had always had the dream and desire for family, but I just never knew fellowship existed to this extent. Family for me has been a group of people that know who God says they are, and know who God is. Family challenges and partners with one another to plow the ground in order to see one another's dreams come true. I truly had never seen or heard of something like this before I came to Isla Vista, and it is one of the main reasons why I love this city so much.

I really believe that there are thousands of people in this city who already have the dream and desire to be loved by God and come into family. We are just part of the process of affirming the revelation of the Holy Spirit that is already in their hearts.

One night at Jesus Burgers I ran into a guy with this kind of revelation. We were in the middle of the street doing a fire tunnel for the students walking by. For those of you who do not know what a fire tunnel is, it is simply two lines of people creating a tunnel for others to run through and praying over each person as they pass by. The party-goers really love it, while unknowingly being touched by God and His love. This particular time, a group of students decided to join us in creating the tunnel, unaware of what really happens.

One of the guys from this group was standing next to me in the tunnel, and we kept laughing together at the people running through and making jokes, and then he looks at me and says, "Can I ask you a question?" He then says, "Do you ever think that people are walking up and down this street searching for something way bigger than parties?" Shocked, I respond by saying that I think that is exactly what they are doing. I went on that I think they are searching for something way bigger than themselves, and that they all just want to be loved for who they really are. He then proceeds to tell me that he hasn't done any drugs or drank alcohol in the last six months because he thinks that being completely coherent is the most exhilarating feeling. He then says, "Do you ever think that everything around us in this world was created for us to enjoy?" By this point, I was trying so hard not to laugh because everything he was saying was clearly from such a Kingdom mindset. He already knew everything that we're taught in the church, but he knew it all from a pure, personal place. The Lord told me while I was talking with him that all he wanted was to be listened to and agreed with. The rest of the world probably thought he was crazy, but I knew he just knew who he was and that he perceived the world rightly from that place.

We ended up talking for about an hour, and not once was there a gap of conversation or an awkward silence. He was just so excited to meet someone that viewed the world similar to him, and didn't think he was crazy for being different. The conversation ended by him saying, "I always look at people's eyes when I'm walking the streets of IV and every time I can see that they are so empty and dark, but when I look in your eyes I see so much light and life. There is something so different about you. What is it that's so different about you?" And it wasn't until then that I knew I could finally explain that Jesus was the reason I see the world similar to him and that Jesus was the reason why I'm so different than other people in this city. Surprisingly, he wasn't even shocked. It was almost as if he knew that this was the truth and the explanation, but no one had ever led him to see it this way. He wasn't offended by it either, but only because I *listened* to him and loved him first, with or without having the same beliefs. He ended up having to leave shortly after that, and he asked if we could ever get together and talk more about things. I told him I would be at the same place every Friday night and I would love to talk more. I haven't seen him since then, but I know that night I watered a seed planted long ago, and all I needed to do was to come into agreement with who he was and what God had *already* been doing in his heart.

Just as God had let me come to Him in His kind, gentle way, letting me realize the desires and beauty that had always been in me, I get to do that for the people on these streets. I get to water the seeds of the desires and revelation He has planted in their hearts and let them realize the truth of who they really are and who He really is. And He causes the growth.

3

I WILL RESTORE TO YOU

RESTORING LIVES FOR MINISTRY

"SO I WILL RESTORE TO YOU THE YEARS THAT THE
SWARMING LOCUST HAS EATEN,
THE CRAWLING LOCUST,
THE CONSUMING LOCUST,
AND THE CHEWING LOCUST,
MY GREAT ARMY WHICH I SENT AMONG YOU."

—*JOEL 2:25 (NKJV)*

God Is Just
That Good

MAC MONTGOMERY

It's quite simple—my story is one of God's goodness manifested in every aspect. He used Jesus
Burgers in Isla Vista to break my heart for a place,
and He brought me the desire to see revival in the
streets of this city.

I was raised in San Diego, California, with some
knowledge of God, but with no clue that I could have
a relationship with Him. I was raised in a home where
the last thing evident was the love and presence of
God. My parents were abusive toward one another, always fighting and screaming. That was my house; that
was my "normal." I thought my parents hated each
other because of me, or I thought that it was my fault
that they couldn't stay together, which brought about
an intense amount of rejection in my heart. I thought
that no one could love me or care for me. Sure, there
were good people around doing good things for me,
but they weren't there late at night when the drunken
rages broke out, or when I cried in my room alone.
They weren't there when I walked into my parents'
fights trying to stop them—only to be ignored—
then watched as they viciously attacked one another,

verbally and physically. I had to find some sort of alternate reality. I couldn't stand who I was or what was happening around me.

My parents split up when I was ten. I was sent to counselors and therapists, but I sat there, silently. None of their book knowledge helped me move from where I was. I lived with extreme depression as a child. I attempted suicide when I was in fifth grade. When that didn't work, all I did was cry, afraid to try again. I was only ten, looking for an escape from this world, looking for the exit door, and finding no release from the pain.

A few years later I was introduced to some temporary escapes. From age thirteen to age sixteen, I scarcely knew a time when I wasn't high or drunk. I was extremely angry and always got into fights and every sort of trouble I could find. When I was fourteen, I got caught for the first time with marijuana at school. It was my third week at this new school, and I got suspended. It was just my luck.

My dad kicked me out of his house in San Diego, and I was sent to live with my mom and stepdad in Santa Barbara. I went through my first drug rehab then, but had no heart change; I went right back into the same old habits. The same thing happened the following year. My mom and stepfather had enough of my lifestyle, so they put me through my second rehab. No heart change. Instead the drug and alcohol abuse continued getting worse and worse. It got to the point where I drank an entire water bottle of vodka before school, then smoked weed, popped pills, and took whatever I could get my hands on to make it through the day, to feel something. One day, however, I had too much, and I threw up all over the halls at school. I was expelled that day—in my junior year in high school, at sixteen years old. The worst part was

I didn't care. Emotionless and apathetic, I had hit a low, low point.

My mom and dad decided to put me in a sober living home run by Calvary Chapel Santa Barbara. I moved in and had to get a job right away, so I was sent to the coffee shop owned by the church. I met a man named Ryan who worked there; he lived in Isla Vista, in the Jesus Burger house. I remember the first day when he said, "Hey, what do you think about Jesus?" And when I said, "I don't know, it's not really my thing," he just smiled and proceeded to befriend me. It was crazy how safe I felt with him.

That weekend after my first week of work, there was a retreat that everyone in the sober living home was going to. I was not looking forward to a weekend with a bunch of weird, old guys talking to me about God. As the first night went by, my heart was as hard as a rock. Then, the second night, Saturday, October 14, 2006, God met me. He said, "My son, I love you. You don't have to try to be strong for yourself anymore; I am here. I have always been here. I never left you, and I never will leave you." He knew that all I needed was my Father's embrace.

I cried for hours, feeling all the weight and pain—all the guilt and shame of a life of sin—lift from me. I was encountering the person of love Himself, and everything was changing. I received His love, and nothing since then has felt the same. I began to see things differently, to feel things differently, and to even smell things differently. I became a brand-new creation. I could take a deep breath without feeling a sense of heaviness in my spirit! I was free! I was alive!

I came back to work that next Monday as a new man: saved, set free, healed, and delivered! I was so in love with Jesus. He came for me when I felt that nobody else would. I couldn't wait to tell my coworker, Ryan.

Ryan became my brother, my best friend. He was twenty-five and I was sixteen, and despite the age difference, he loved me so well. He watched after me and showed me who Jesus was. He invited me out to his house in Isla Vista for Halloween weekend, which was a pretty crazy thing for a sixteen-year-old recovering alcoholic. Here I was, living in a sober living home and going out to one of the craziest party towns in the whole nation on the craziest night of the year! However, I knew why I was going out there; to be a light in the darkness. Little did Ryan know that he was introducing me to my life's calling.

That Halloween was the most incredible thing I had ever been a part of. I was seeing for the first time with new eyes what I was doing before I got saved. Now keep in mind, I had been a Christian for two weeks. I mean, I was fresh off the block and by no means qualified. All I had was Jesus and hope, and that is what I gave away. I saw lives transformed that weekend, and I knew God had said, "This is your city; take it. I am giving it to you."

So I kept coming back. Jesus Burgers was what introduced me to loving the lost. These people who had been doing it for a long time showed me Christ and how He loves people. Now, I'm still here in Isla Vista, called to the city for life, to contend for revival in the streets and revolutionize the city with the worship our church is producing. I am now the worship pastor of our church and am recording and producing worship albums that come out of Isla Vista. Jesus Burgers is what started it all.

It has been six years since that first weekend, and my life has only gotten better and more glorious along the way. I have seen so many lives completely changed, and I've seen so many miracles happen on the street right in front of Jesus Burgers. However, there is one story I want to share in particular—a story that is still unfolding—it is one of the most amazing things I have ever experienced. This is the story of one changed life, a person I will call "Sonny" instead of using his real name.

I met Sonny a long time ago. I was a leader at the high school worship group that he showed up at from time to time. The first time I ever saw him, God spoke as clear as day, "I have anointed him with fire." I was taken aback.

It's shocking sometimes to see people the way God sees them. God lifted the veil off of my eyes so I would see him from heaven's perspective, and I saw this glorious warrior covered in fire—darkness was petrified of him. I fell in love with the little surf grom; he was my homie. And he was hungry for God. I have never met someone who loves worship as much. However, I knew that outside of church it was really hard; all his friends were gnarly druggies, and he was stuck in it. I was a friend for him whenever he needed someone to come to. There was a period of time after that when I didn't see him too often. He had slipped back into the party scene again. But one night, after not seeing him for a long time, I saw him at Jesus Burgers, and things changed for Sonny.

It was a wild night in Isla Vista. The DJ across the street blared crazy trance techno and dubstep. You could feel the heavy intensity and darkness in the air. All around us drunken guys and girls threw themselves at each other, looking for some sort of fulfillment and satisfaction. I stood on the balcony of the Jesus Burgers house, watching people walk back and forth as if they were zombies—they looked like they had no sense of hope or direction, just doing it for the sake of doing it.

It seemed like it was going to be one of those nights

when we wouldn't really able to do much other than give a couple burgers away, until I saw him. Sonny was walking down the street with the rest of the thousands of people. I felt this thing rise up in me, this radical hope well up inside me, like I wouldn't just be going to say hey to him. He was already a half block away when I decided to run downstairs. With the music blasting I could barely hear myself think, let alone talk, but I yelled out his name as loud as I could from a block away. He heard it and stopped dead in his tracks. He turned around and saw me standing there, and tears began to stream down his face.

In the middle of Isla Vista on his way to a party, with all of his friends standing there, he began to cry. We stood there for what seemed to be an eternity, locking eyes. I smiled and he cried harder. As I ran toward him and embraced him, he said, "What is happening? I saw you and I started to feel the presence of God. It was like all those times we would worship together came back to me. The moment I saw you I felt love and peace. I couldn't handle it because I'm partying, and I feel like such a hypocrite." I said, "Dude, God loves you that much that He wanted to encounter you in the last place you would expect! You would never expect to encounter God in Isla Vista while you're partying, but He wanted you that bad that He couldn't wait any longer. He wanted you now." Sonny continued to cry.

I put my arm around him, and we walked back to the Jesus Burger house. Everyone at the house came to us and surrounded him with hugs and love. It was like he was finally home.

Jesus met him in the street that night, and He used us to do it. Sonny still comes around every now and then; he's figuring out everything for himself. For some it's a one-time encounter, and for others it may be a five-year process—but Sonny has come home for good. I know he has. That night changed everything in his life. After bringing him back to the Jesus Burger house, we went inside and worshiped for hours like we used to. We stayed up until four or five in the morning talking and worshiping together. He was amazed with how good God was. He said over and over how things would never be the same. He confessed all this sin in his life, repented, and returned to Jesus that night. Since then, I have seen him a few times here and there, and every time he gives me the biggest hug because he knows that when he is ready, there is a family of believers in Isla Vista who will love him and take him in with open arms.

That is Jesus Burgers for you. It isn't the actual event that changes people, but it's the people that are a part of it. Love is what changes people. It changed my life, and now I get to be a part of the cycle and watch more lives transformed by God's love overflowing through me. God is just that good.

GOD PLACES THE LONELY IN FAMILIES

JOSEPH GRANADO

People are looking for somewhere to belong. Community. Family. I know I was. That's what I saw when I first came to Isla Vista Church and Jesus Burgers. It was exactly what I needed.

Since my teenage years growing up in Lake Arrowhead, California, I had sought fulfillment, satisfaction, identity, and self-worth in worthless and barren places. Like many of the students in Isla Vista, I tapped into partying, drugs, and alcohol. I selfishly forged relationships to make me feel like I was worth something and was loved by others. I considered myself to be a "good person" and used that disguise as an all-access pass to do whatever I wanted.

God used my good friends Baron and Jen Santos to draw me into His family. In the community of believers in Isla Vista, I met God in a powerful, life-altering way. Through His people, the Church, and their love (which begins and flows out of Him), God wrecked my whole view of life and my crummy plan for happiness.

Baron and Jen shared with me about what God was doing in Isla Vista. They didn't force anything on me, but just shared their excitement and enthusiasm. I was intrigued. It sparked a curiosity in my soul that made me want to investigate. I ended up inviting myself to their church service one Sunday.

When I got to the church, I was welcomed into a beautiful community, one unlike anything I had experienced before. I felt the sense of family, the care for one another's hearts and dreams, passions and pains. I couldn't believe how bold the preacher, Jacob Reeve, was in proclaiming the truth about things like pornography, lust, and sex outside of the commitment of marriage!

Hearing the truth and learning what God says is right and wrong "ruined" me for good. I couldn't keep living the way I had been. I broke up with my girlfriend and began to seek God more and more.

I started coming to Jesus Burgers in 2004. It was here at this weekend barbecue that God started showing me about how He wired me. I began to realize that my job in the restaurant/hospitality industry wasn't just a job but a gifting from God that could be used to touch people's lives.

It was soon after this that I moved into the Jesus Burgers house. I was immersed in a culture of family like never before. It was here that I began to play a bigger part in Jesus Burgers, taking on the grilling as my main role in the evening. Eventually, I became the main overseer of the night, from purchasing the hamburger meat and supplies to cooking and handing out the hamburgers at Jesus Burgers each week.

Over the years, I have been continually amazed at the reaction we get from handing out these seriously simple and inexpensive treats: nothing fancy, just bun, ketchup, mustard, and patty. That's it! People are shocked that we would want to give away free burgers to complete strangers. The fact that we are willing to open our house, cook up a delicious burger, and give it away for free opens up people's hearts to experience the love of God. We are able to meet, talk with, care for, and befriend all kinds of people. We are not there to force anything on anyone, but we are definitely there if someone has questions about God, Jesus, the Bible, life, love, anything!

Unfortunately, in 2006, after a couple of years living at the Jesus Burgers house, I fell back into drinking and using drugs. Even though I was seeking God and trying to live my life for Him, I never addressed the issues that I had in my heart or the fact that I had started abusing substances when I was fifteen. There was almost ten years of junk built up inside me that had never been cleaned out.

I ended up falling pretty hard into drugs and alcohol again and came to a point where I was about to lose everything: my job was in jeopardy, my finances jacked up, my health was failing, and I was on the verge of losing my closest friends as I was pushing everyone away from me. Thank God that I had friends who cared enough and were willing to stand up and confront me in my darkest hour. They mapped out the two paths I had before me: on the one hand, I could continue down my dark path of self-destruction, or I could choose life and get help. I was persuaded to forsake the path that would lead to my demise and was able to choose life!

Over the next couple of years, God showed me the places in my heart and head that needed healing, and I was actually able to receive deep healing and get free from addiction. He also showed me that I am valuable to Him and that He has a plan and a purpose for my life. I could finally see some of the biggest blessings had been right in front of me for a long time. My eyes were opened to see the woman

God would have me marry (as it turns out she was a part of Isla Vista Church and Jesus Burgers, and we had been friends for a few years already). I ended up pursuing her, and we got married in 2009.

I am still learning what it means to be a son of God and a godly husband, as well as how to lead people and oversee whatever God has entrusted to me in a way that gives Him glory. I am convinced that there is hope for anyone who is trapped in addiction, loneliness, or has a broken heart. God is able to deliver us from all these things by placing us in His family where we can learn to be His children. This to me is what Jesus Burgers is about; it is about offering a city hope for whatever they are facing today. Jesus is that hope, and the love behind these hamburgers has been that hope to me. I am so thankful for the family of God, and I am excited to see how God is going to continue to use us to love a city, one hamburger at a time.

"Father to the fatherless, defender of widows — this is God, whose dwelling is holy. God places the lonely in families; he sets the prisoners free and gives them joy" (Psalm 68:5–6 NLT).

THE ONE

KRISSY MASON

It was senior year of high school. Going to college was yet another one of those "big deal" things that bred all sorts of insecurity in me. My friends were all talking about their plans for universities, goals, and commitments, which led to my automatic series of smiles and nods. By this point in my life, I had gotten really good at smiling and nodding. I had smiled and nodded in my small town while I tried to hold it together after the death of my sister. I had smiled and nodded through my parents' divorce. I had smiled and nodded through years of cutting myself and a five-year-long battle of anorexia and bulimia. Everything was erupting under the surface, but I continued to smile and nod my life away. I look back and think about how much I thought I had fooled everyone with how well I was doing or how popular and together I was, when the real truth was I was a deteriorating mess. I was spiraling downward on the inside with haunting depression, while battling voices of hate and rejection.

I wanted out. I was sick of "being okay." I was sick of hating myself, my family, and God. I don't think I would have known a real relationship if it screamed at me. My best friends changed every week; I could barely keep track of who I was supposed to hate and who hated me. Awesome.

So, high school was a bust, what's new? It kind of goes that way for most. For me, however, I was stuck in a trap of lies. For a lengthy portion of my life, I felt that I was unwanted, unloved, and unnoticed. Everything was fake.

It was finally senior year, and I was going to get out. I had made it through high school with most of the really horrible things hidden while maintaining the status quo: decent popularity and a cheating boyfriend. I had somehow managed to escape the drugs and keep my virginity. I also had a tiny bit of hope that lingered in my heart from a Young Life camp or two. At that time in my life, that's what I called living victoriously. The next plan was a forward march to college to become something—to become anything different than what I had been faking for most of my life. My plan was to kick the eating disorder and to become normal by having an amazing partying, drinking, and experimental four years as far away from home and everyone else that carried any aroma of my adolescent years as possible.

Santa Barbara, California: where I arrived for college a week after I graduated. I carried my independent and slightly rotting soul to Isla Vista. I really did think things would be different. I thought I could get over who had hurt me and why I hurt myself, but the never-ending desperation to be needed and wanted transformed me into a girl I never thought I would be. I used to make fun of these girls: the ones who so obviously found their identity in men and being attractive. Now I see it was a slow deterioration because of my insecurities, loneliness, and near zero self-worth.

It all crept up on me so sneakily, so deceivingly.

I always felt that I was supposed to be important, like Hollywood important. Isla Vista has a way about it that, for one night, you can be fooled into thinking you're a movie star. Little did I know I was always important to God and that He sacrificed His Son just to lavish me with love.

With long blonde hair extensions, short dresses, high heels, and an addiction to Adderall, I fit into Isla Vista pretty brilliantly. You can create entire party events around yourself knowing almost everyone in the whole city if you are pretty enough or probably more accurately, easy enough. I remember laughing with my friends every weekend morning about things like accidentally hooking-up with the same guy because we were so drunk or high, or reflecting on how we watched some guy eat glass because of the trip he was on. Back then we referred to one another as slut or bitch as a sign of endearment. This was my life. I didn't even recognize myself. How did I become this person?

I was a good girl who let the principalities of the city work their way into my already wounded heart. The numbness only intensified while the smiling and nodding became my agreements with the devil. I would wake up shivering and vomiting most mornings, but not from alcohol; instead, it was from my nerves. I would make myself sick to my stomach with the decisions I had made the night before—only hating myself even more for it the next day. Of course, I explained my sickness to my roommates as a hangover.

I remember just longing to be married, to be picked, to have another escape from this season of life and to be taken away, far away, from this masochistic trap I kept enduring. If I were married I wouldn't be a slave anymore to impressing men sexually. I wouldn't be a slave anymore to my tan, hair extensions, or skinny body. Maybe I just wouldn't be a slave at all. Something about that idea of marriage brought safety, protection, and freedom to my heart. I was a bride yearning for her bridegroom. I wanted to be "the one" and find my one.

In a word, I was hungry. Starving in fact: physically and spiritually. I think my body just followed my soul's state. It was a reflection of what I needed: intense intervention and nourishment from the One and Only Jesus Christ. My heart was screaming for Jesus to come and marry me, and the time was ripe.

I was the girl we all testify about now; the girl who came to Jesus Burgers and talked about God and sang the worship songs around the bonfire. We'll say something like, "She was drunk, but she was singing the songs. Praise God!" I was the girl walking by Jesus Burgers in provocative clothing hanging on some guy saying, "Oh yeah, I don't need the gospel. I know Jesus." That was the problem. I might have known the gospel and known who Jesus was, but I didn't know love, and I didn't know He was the ONLY source of the greatest love ever known.

After I lived over a year in this destructive lifestyle, God brought me to ultimate brokenness and fatigue. He began to do major heart surgery. I moved out of IV only to have Him call me back a couple years later, saved and redeemed. This sent me on a 180-degree journey back to grasp little girls who were like me and place them into Jesus' arms. This time I was standing on the other side of Del Playa, facing those girls with the small skirts, glazed eyes, and empty souls eager to have them meet my new friend, husband, and lover of my soul, Jesus Christ.

Living outside of IV with my heart on the mend, I was serving at a college ministry where I initially got saved. "From everyone who has been given much, much will be required" (Luke 12:48). I knew there was a greater destiny available to me in God that I hadn't fully understood yet. I had heard about Jesus Burgers through this ministry, and I remember laughing as I reflected on my days there being the receiver. I had mixed feelings about attending now as a Christian. Would my old drunk friends recognize me? Would these Jesus people recognize me as the way I was before? I went anyway, and it became a habit from there on out.

The first time I went I met Jason, the pastor, and now my spiritual father. I'll never forget how he encouraged me that God was calling me to sit and rest and learn to be a daughter. A daughter? It was powerful for me that a random person would seek me out to pray over me and share encouragement from heaven. This began a journey that sent me into the next three years of my life dedicated to the city, learning how to be a daughter and point other future daughters to their Father in heaven.

I knew I had found the place where God wanted me. I have had several conversations with girls who were like me over the years at Jesus Burgers. I was so hungry to see someone fully transformed by His love the way that I had been. We got to prophesy, tell girls who they really were in God's eyes, and generally just love on them. The excitement to see change only increased every time someone was led to tears by the Father's heart over them. It made me want more.

I wanted God to give me one girl to help. I wanted a life that I could pour out on to all God had given me. I would pray often, "Come on, God, give me one, just one girl, to turn from these ways and come into the family." I never felt discouraged praying and loving on people into the late nights; something glorious always manifested and pointed to Jesus every night. Whether there was salvation or not, He was glorified.

Then there was this very special night that a girl with her boyfriend came inside to the girls' house up-stairs, away from the darkness, the crowds, and the lost, and came into the light: a room full of people who were full of Jesus and ready to get to her heart. Prophesying over this girl changed my life. I have never have felt the heart of God so strongly. Looking at her was like looking in a mirror; it was so easy to love her because I could feel that she was just as trapped and lost in the ways of the world that I once had been. That's what Jesus Burgers is to me: sharing the heart of Father God and the sacrifice of His son for His people as we are led by the Holy Spirit.

God gives us specific vision, insight, wisdom, and counsel for each person He loves. He never misses, and He is always right. There were about ten of us in the room that night speaking life into her as she tried to take it all in. She was God's.

In many cases, you might not ever see the per-son you witnessed to again, but when people disap-pear, God never does. His Spirit was with that girl, continuing to woo her. I am never disappointed that people don't come to salvation right away, because we have hope. Ministering at Jesus Burgers means we get to carry hope and life for people who don't know how to hope for themselves. I didn't know if I would see that girl ever again. I just left with hope that she saw Jesus and felt his love that night. But God honored my prayer when she came around again. He brought her back to me, and we got to sit and cry together, yet again, as God allowed me to pour out the life He had given me into her. We kneeled, prayed, and wept together a year later from that powerful night we met at Jesus Burgers. I knew during that second visit that it was over for her; God had brought her to the same place I once was: to brokenness.

She was ready, and it was His perfect plan and timing. Her life in the world was over, and God took the old and made her a new creation.

It's funny, because I might have been teaching her things and helping her with her new life with Jesus, but the truth was, I have never learned more about God's love than when I saw Him sweep her off her feet and turn her into a radical worshiper of Jesus. The fact that He used me gave me more life than I had ever known. I watched His miracles of love wash her clean, and it was the most beautiful thing I had ever witnessed. I am still close to her and so proud of her. I asked for one girl to bring to Jesus, and I got her! Now this girl is giving that same love back to others, and I have seen several come to know Jesus because of her new life in Him.

That's what Jesus Burgers is about. It expresses the heart for the one. He leaves the hundred to go after the one. The wonderful thing about God is that everyone is "the one" on that night, and we get to be the hands and feet for Him. It's about giving back what you've been given so that more and more people can get set free from the bondage of this world and adopted into the Kingdom. He transformed me so I could transform others, and so it continues. It will continue to be that way until we see the new Heaven and the new Earth—and for me it started at Jesus Burgers.

THE GIFT
OF FAMILY

DANIEL HAYRAPETIAN

Inhale the smoke of burning weed in a piece of crafted glass. Chomp on a four-dollar In-N-Out double-double burger. Repeat. This is how I enjoyed the final days of summer before leaving for college. I would soon make a new home at the University of California, Santa Barbara: the holy grail of girls and substances. The years people esteem as the best of their lives drew closer that summer with each puff and each burger bite.

On my first night out in Isla Vista, I stumbled into a social that a club was having at Starbucks for new freshmen. As I discovered an unusual amount of Christians in the greeting crew, uneasiness made its entrance and signaled to my stomach to turn over relentlessly. Uh oh, I thought. Religion sucks. I need to get out of here. Before leaving, however, something compelled me to ridicule the Christians. I coolly asked one, "So why do you believe?"

He told the story of how Jesus changed his life. A heavy, tingling sensation pulsated through my body. I felt unsure of what that sensation was, but feelings of reassurance from an unknown origin rooted themselves deep in my heart—confirming the moment's goodness and safeness.

In the days following, I stumbled through the streets of Isla Vista publicly intoxicated, and I attempted to wrap my mind around that night. My thoughts abruptly came to a halt.

"Get up," said a group of three men shining a flashlight in my eyes. "What are you doing down there?"

Struggling to respond, I attempted to plead my case, "mmm . . . mah friends . . . yeah . . . they. . . .'re com . . .ing. . . . yeah." While I thought I had pulled off a great performance, the puddles of vomit around me ratted me out.

"All right, let's take this kid in." After a series of tugs, pulls, and stumbles, the police put me in their squad car and intimately acquainted me with the city drunk tank for the next twenty hours.

Oh no. no, no no no no nooo . . . What am I going to do. I'm in big trouble, my parents are going to kill me. I'm not going to be able to get a job. I buried my face into my hands and sobbed as waves of hopelessness, emptiness, and helplessness confronted and overcame me.

My mind wandered to that guy's story about Jesus. If He had changed that guy's entire life, then maybe Jesus could do the same thing for me.

Clutching this tiny yet strangely captivating kernel of hope, I desperately said to God, "I don't know what life with you looks like, but if you will drop these charges, I will give you my life." In that instant, He answered my plea: the police told me they dropped the charges. I had only to pay a small fine. This sign awoke my heart for God.

After my release, I returned to my daily life with a desire to know Jesus more. With a child-like simplicity, I realized that those who followed Jesus could tell me about Him. My search led me to attend a Campus Crusade (known as Real Life at UCSB) retreat where, during a time of worship, I cried my heart dry as God orchestrated an invasion of love in my heart and toppled the idols of my old life. The chorus repeated in my heart, "And the cry of my heart is to bring you praise, from the inside out, Lord, my soul cries out!" In that moment, I gave my life to Jesus and everything changed.

Over the next seven months, God took my countless shortcomings and brokenness and exchanged them for a myriad of life and beauty. Like any transformative endeavor, it was messy. I bobbed between learning new truths in the Bible and returning to the party lifestyle, yet the seed of faith within me continued to grow with God's grace.

One weekend I partied with an old high school friend. He rejected what little bit I attempted to share with him about Jesus. This encounter opened my eyes to the discrepancy between my life and the life Jesus called me to live. This prompted me to let the old man—the life I lived before knowing Jesus—die in the cold waters of the Pacific Ocean: I was baptized as a follower of Christ. Shortly after this event, my story with God entered into a new arc when I was invited to live in the Jesus Burgers home.

"You guys do what, now?" I responded in shock when I first heard Pastor Jason Lomelino's radical vision for a Christian community in IV. I could not have guessed that my acceptance of his invitation would push me into season after season of the most tremendous growth in my faith.

The DP House, commonly referred to as the Jesus Burgers house, consists of a community of seven guys downstairs, and seven girls living in the upstairs unit. "If it weren't for God, I would probably not have lived with these guys," has been a phrase to describe the hilarity of how God could grow this group of people with a laughable amount of difference in personality and taste into a close family.

Many of the transformative experiences in the house were often masked as challenges and obstacles. "Hey, you guys, clean your dishes after you use 'em! Frick!" expressed a frustrated house member. Cleaning stacks of housemates' dirty dishes twice a day for a week tends to be an open invitation for the selfishness in our hearts to express unhealthy attitudes toward one another. Yet, God has a way of freeing the heart from that place of bitterness and anger, while filling us with understanding that service is simply storing up treasures in heaven, pouring into us His love for our housemates, and giving us joy in freely giving away one's time and energy.

Time spent together as brothers and sisters allows God to craft a heart of family and love in the house. In spite of the busyness of college, the group intentionally meets monthly to share a meal together.

"We made a quinoa medley, home fries, and homemade chili for the potluck. Good huh?" the girls said proudly.

"We bought eight servings of macaroni salad from the store and brought a half-baked loaf of cornbread," said the guys in a similar pride.

"Wait . . . What? Gross!" the girls responded half chuckling, half trying to figure out what would compel us to buy that unnecessary amount of macaroni salad. The girls, being somewhat conscious about healthy food choices, would not eat the amorphous blob of macaroni salad, and it was clear the guys were completely oblivious. Laughter ensued and bonds formed.

Furthermore, the lives of the people in the Jesus

Burgers house have become channels for the greatest sermons I've ever heard. The insights and revelations shared are some of the deepest and most profound I know. The voice of a friend struggling with lust as he weeps, "I don't know what to do but to just trust Him that He will give me new desires," reverberates louder than any exegetical expansion of Psalm 37:4.

Through their many lives, I learned to remain faithful, support people's dreams, encourage their faith, love them like Jesus would, and share the totality of life with my brothers and sisters. As God filled our hearts and lives with His extravagant love, our natural response was to share this gift of family and love with the city of Isla Vista.

"Can we use your bathroom? Please? We know Scotty lives here; he said we could." A group of five girls came to Jesus Burgers after eleven thirty at night hoping to use our restroom.

Chuckling, I responded, "Uh . . . there isn't a Scotty who lives here, but you are more than welcome to use our bathroom." We were happy to oblige.

"Oh, wow! Thank you so much! You guys are so nice!" They promptly rushed inside. All five of them piled into our tiny bathroom. The sole male friend of theirs propped himself on the leather couches and words of thankfulness flowed from his mouth. "Yeah, you guys are the sh*t—thanks so much for letting them use it." (The expletive in that context is actually a compliment.) "The girls were driving me crazy and were going to pee in the streets."

Joy filled the room as he attempted to convey his thankfulness for the uncommon gesture of offering our bathroom. Conversation turned deeper as I asked him about his life and listened to his story. A myriad of hurt, love, pain, depression, hope, and hopelessness covered the canvas of his life, and God's love for him moved me to plant a seed of hope as I reassured him that God lives today and Jesus transformed my life. He thanked me for the story and left with his friends.

This scenario repeats itself about three to five times every week at Jesus Burgers. Eyes bulge, mouths drop, and smiles ensue when drunken strangers hear they are welcome in our home. Whether it's a brief pit stop, a warm place to pass out, or a safe space to share the inner workings of their hearts, the Jesus Burgers house serves as a refuge for those in Isla Vista. In an average month, we host about two thousand partiers, serve six hundred free burgers, offer our restrooms for use, and drive home about five students who blacked-out from drinking too much. Not to mention that we have hundreds of conversations with students and out-of-town visitors who party in the streets almost every night.

One night at the conclusion of the last Jesus Burgers barbecue of the school year, I noticed that the atmosphere seemed mellow and peaceful. Wandering into the house, I saw a tall, Hispanic student with a freshly lined fade slumped on our couch—with his eyes closed, mouth open, and head supported by an unopened roll of Kirkland paper towels.

"He's our friend from the army," one of his three buddies told us. "We wanted to show him a good time. I guess it was a little too good." One of his friends placed a hand on his forehead while another helped him toward a garbage bag offered by one of our housemates.

"Thanks so much for letting him sit here until he sobers up," they said. We assured them that it was no problem and asked them about their stories. In between moments of helping the young man expel the beer and vodka, we found out that one of them had

faith in God and loved Jesus. We spoke encouragement over him and affirmed the truth of God's love
for him and the freedom Jesus gives.

The three were overflowing with thanks, apolo-
gizing unnecessarily as our love met their guilt.
Warmness bubbled in my heart as I saw them giving
thanks and realizing that without God's help, their
intoxicated friend would not have made it home.

"You guys just love well," said one of their friends
as they stood to leave. "We feel loved here. Thank you
so much."

Without the love of God we experience in our DP
house family on a daily basis, Jesus Burgers would
not have a place to serve from and all these stories
would not exist. Praise God for family.

Isla Vista, you are cordially invited into the family
of God.

FOUND A
BETTER PARTY

IAN KING

Although raised in a Christian home, I rebelled against nearly the entirety of everything I had been taught, especially when it came to the topic of Jesus. During my sophomore year of high school, I took on the label of being Christian, but in actuality my lifestyle hardly changed: I continued partying, getting drunk, and hooking up with girls. It was only after I stopped partying for a few weekends that I became aware of the void I had been trying to fill. Despite my attempts to fill this void, it continued to grow.

After high school, I came to Santa Barbara to attend Santa Barbara City College and quickly became introduced to the infamous party scene of Isla Vista. I met some people who offered me a near-identical lifestyle to my high school experience. I found myself again claiming to be a Christian, yet indulging in every IV experience available. Over the course of a year and a half, I would walk the streets of DP (Del Playa) from party to party while trying to avoid the Jesus Burgers house, where there were people I knew and went to church with at Reality. My sense of shame prevented me from even getting near the Jesus Burgers house. While I felt convicted over my lack of integrity, I never confronted myself. I simply refused to give up the "fun" that I was addicted to. I effectively lived a double life: I regularly went to church, Bible studies, men's groups, college groups, and worship nights. Beyond my perfect attendance, however, my life continued to be dominated by the same growing void that my partying could not satisfy.

One night at a local college group, God broke me down. I distinctly remember hearing His voice telling me, "You cannot live this life. It is spiritually destroying you and everyone around you." He then gave me an ultimatum, saying, "Either choose Me or the world, because you cannot have both." I'd never heard the voice of God so clearly and so tangibly; it was as if there was a physical person speaking directly in my ears. Realizing I could no longer ignore God, I broke down in tears, resolving to truly commit my life to the Lord. God lead me to Hebrews 6:19, which tells us, "This hope is a strong and trustworthy anchor for our souls. It leads us through the curtain into God's inner sanctuary." This verse has continued to this day to challenge and encourage me. Previously, my faith could best be likened to a roller coaster: one day I would love God and follow Him and be up so high, but the next day I would plummet down into my sin and stay there. I was a vessel with no anchor, drifting farther and farther from the shore and farther and farther from God's glory.

Shortly after committing my life fully to Jesus and realizing the reality of being anchored in Christ, I again found myself at Jesus Burgers with some of my friends from church. Only this time I was no longer ashamed of myself. Instead, I found myself serving burgers to my old party friends, who now wanted nothing to do with me because I wasn't coming to their parties anymore.

It was then that I realized that our friendships lacked substance. They didn't value me for who I was, but for the entertainment I could provide them. I tried to explain to my friends how I had found satisfaction and true happiness, but they neither understood nor cared.

The profound difference between the party community and the Christian community became apparent chiefly because of the organic love and genuine care the latter gave me. At Isla Vista Church and Jesus Burgers, I found a community committed to genuinely loving and caring for one another. That is why we call it a family. Good families accept one another for who they are. They not only embrace each other in the midst of failures but also work through failure so that they may overcome.

When I was partying, I didn't realize I was merely searching to satisfy an unquenchable thirst. All those things were momentary and never once gave me true satisfaction. The lifestyle I found in IV did have a deceptive appeal, but the reality is the party lifestyle cannot accomplish the full measure of what God has planned for us. He took my broken past—filled with drinking, sex, smoking, and cursing His name—and He showed me love. I thought I had to clean up my life before coming to Him. I learned, however, He simply wanted me to be real with Him and share my heart, so that He could comfort and restore me.

I also had a mindset in which I imagined I couldn't both love a stern and serious God and enjoy my life. Like so many others, I construed God to be a big stoic judge, constantly preventing people from having fun lest they sin. I had this ridiculous outlook before God just took my partying and purified it, smothered it in joy and His love, and told me to dance. I never knew how joyful and fulfilling partying with God could be. One of the most important parts of life with God, I've found, comes from fully realizing the joy that comes from enjoying Him.

After attending Isla Vista Church and Jesus Burgers, I finally moved to IV from Santa Barbara, now with the new purpose of becoming part of my new loving family. With this fresh inspiration, I played worship songs on Friday nights at Jesus Burgers in front of thousands of people walking the streets, and dancing and singing in the rain on Halloween. As I got more involved with Jesus Burgers, I started to help make the burgers; I got more and more opportunities to love on people by talking with them and praying for them. I have had the most real and authentic experiences with God at Jesus Burgers and the Upper Room, complete with fully satisfying love and encouragement from those around me.

Before coming to IVC and Jesus Burgers, I had never encountered a church family that genuinely loved and looked out for one another. My prior idea of Christians was characterized by fake smiles and judgmental looks. At IVC, I have only seen genuine love and sincere encouragement through hard times, whether the love is shown through prayer, tears, or both. And everything I have experienced in this community has encouraged me to continue to grow.

God spoke His will into my life. My usefulness to God and what He has me do on this earth was something I had always wondered, and at times, worried about. I have always had a soft heart and cared for people and their well being. The Lord had consistently and tangibly told me that He wanted me to be a pastor and to shepherd His people. Although I actually had a few thoughts about this in high school,

I never wanted to pursue it until I found the realness of God's love and power.

He works on hearts and has turned a hedonistic partier into His servant. My Savior killed that old sinful life and gave me a new life and a new purpose—to be entrusted today to tend and feed His sheep.

Quite recently, God has called me to be a pastor, and has called me specifically to IVC. This is a testimony about the power of God, how strong His love is, and how strong His work is.

The Jesus Burgers ministry through IVC has had such a huge impact on my whole life. It is the hub of encouragement and love. It is a bunch of people who love the Lord and love each other, hanging out and championing one another every weekend. This love that I've felt firsthand from the ministry has spurred me on to grow closer to God and, in turn, to spur on others as well.

Now I am an anchored vessel, not drifting, but steadfast, no matter how hard the winds blow.

CAPTIVATING THE HEART

ROBBY BUSTAMANTE

In boxing, trainers often go to great lengths to inculcate their fighters with the saying, "Take out the body and the head will follow." Simply put, this strategy stresses the need for the fighter to take out the body of his opponent rather than giving in to the seemingly intuitive approach of attacking his head to knock him out and take the fight.

Both my testimony and my time at the Jesus Burgers house has lead me to believe that this principle is equally effective and aptly employed by the Lord in the contest for our hearts and minds. He relentlessly pursues us and subsequently overcomes us, not through the head via an intellectual exercise, but instead through the body by captivating the heart. While we are so often captivated by testimonies defined by a single moment of epiphany, my faith in Jesus occurred gradually as He overcame me through conversations, relationships, and radical encounters of true freedom in His presence.

My life prior to coming to the Jesus Burgers house could best be described as a calculated attempt to understand myself and find meaning reactively and purely through my intellect. Although I had everything I could ask of my family—a good name and unqualified love—abuse, mainly vocal but sometimes physical, undeniably shaped the thematic overtones of my life narrative. I distinctly remember one exact moment, during a particularly brutal fight, when I watched myself in the third person as I emotionally shut down and simply killed off that caring, hoping part of myself to stop the hurting. For years after that single moment, the entirety of my personal drive and mentality became one-dimensionally consumed by an anger that pushed me to become smarter, stronger, and more successful solely for a single purpose. I remember that in such emotional callousness and numbness, I would methodically and calmly remind myself before falling asleep each night, "As soon as I'm big enough and old enough, this will never happen again." While I had embraced an idea of God and Christianity from the lens of my Catholic upbringing and then through the lens of a Christian private school, I fundamentally lacked the emotional will and capacity to see what it had to do with me. I could rationalize and argue for or against Him all that I wanted, but I had no substantive experience to speak for. Depression, "that black dog," rattled me to my core as I increasingly saw the emptiness of my quality of life and my own utter inability to find substantive meaning and purpose.

For me, coming to Santa Barbara and particularly encountering the IVC and Jesus Burgers folks in Isla Vista catalyzed something within me. Above all, I became captivated by the stark contrast between living for the Lord and living for oneself. Whereas so often we can become cathartic in pervasive gray areas of attempting to live right to some degree, yet also pursuing our pleasure, and ourselves, Isla Vista blatantly allowed me to see the full trajectory of what pursuing such an empty existence entailed. Here, I realized, the widely diverse group of young minds that come to this quintessentially collegiate neighborhood are presented with every opportunity to experience the alleged pinnacle of what the world has to offer. In actuality, the deceptive allure of Isla Vista serves as a thin mask over its deeply pervasive violence, sexual brokenness, and substance abuse. The sheer scale of this brokenness quickly became wildly apparent to me, especially through the near-constant roar of ambulances and fire trucks weaving through the crowded streets of the neighborhood, ferrying away those who have in essence destroyed themselves in attempting to realize some conception of the good life. It was in this dark and anarchic neighborhood that I was able to see the true beauty and power of a Christ-centered community characterized by genuine love and passionately devoted to the service of others, even though they seemingly appear to be outfunded, outmanned, and outmatched.

As my preconceived notions and supposed knowledge of Christianity crumbled under the weight of experiencing simple truths clearly silhouetted against the absurdity of the surrounding spectacle, I for the first time began to live life abundantly. Indeed, I was stunned to see my anger give way to peace as the mosaic of my life now became enveloped by themes such as the Father's love, the perfect romance of Christ and the church, and the transcendent peace and rest in the Holy Spirit. My decision to live at the Jesus Burgers house and join Isla Vista Church eminently enhanced and guided my transformation of the heart. In addition to having experienced the most satisfying intimacy, fellowship, and mentorship within this community, I have wept uncontrollably. I have been stretched beyond my capacity, fought and argued with the Lord, and experienced pain, physical and emotional. Regardless, I consider these experiences invaluable because they are above all genuinely substantive, for I have been fortunate enough to experience such a wide range of life's triumphs and challenges in community rather than living merely for my own needs and enjoyment.

I have found C. S. Lewis' conception of the church as an underground resistance movement taking part in a great campaign of sabotage amidst enemy-occupied territory particularly apt of our movement. And in this invasion, the Spirit of God moves forcefully and eloquently, healing the sick and injured as He calls out the true identities of those who have known only deception. One episode I recall—that to me encapsulates the heart behind Jesus Burgers and the simple yet profoundly transformative impact it has in extending the kingdom of God—began as we were grilling one Friday night. An unkempt and somewhat drunk fellow named Jorge approached me with a forty-ounce beer in his right hand. He repeatedly told us he was amazed that people served one another in such a way, and further, that he wanted to help us with the grill. We obliged him, and after he had spent the night in our company laughing and mingling with all those whom we got to serve, we moved into the living room. I casually asked if Jorge wanted to tell me more about his life, and I soon learned he had immigrated to Santa Barbara from Mexico. While he did have family in the neighboring town of Carpinteria, they had not spoken in years due to a family fight. Jorge went on to confess that he was completely alone, addicted to alcohol, and unable to work as he had lost his visa and employment papers two weeks prior. I'll never forget how he began to burst into tears as he muttered, "Nobody knows my name."

In that moment of true vulnerability, I hugged him and wept with him over the deception that had caused him so much pain. A few others and myself spent the next hour affirming Jorge in prayer and encouraging him by speaking fresh promises over him. Still half crying, he told us he had decided he would travel to his estranged family in Carpinteria to make things right and start anew. Although I never had the opportunity to see him again after I bought him his bus tickets back to Carp, I do remember that Saturday morning when I found the forty-ounce bottle in our living room, which he had tellingly left as he went on his way to reconnect with his family. I believe it is in this fashion that we are called to love on others: through listening, serving, and encouraging, rather than lecturing or arguing.

My entire life—who I am and who I aspire to be—can be framed through my time at Jesus Burgers on nights such as these. At the house, I've been privileged to cultivate an exceptional vibrancy of life, holding an intrinsic value I formerly could only distantly conceive. Although these seasons of spiritual growth have been anything but comfortable and easy, they have been inexplicably peaceful and restful. Truly, the quality and character of every facet of my life has been enriched by my time at the house. I'm a better son because He fathers me. I am a better friend because He calls me friend. I am a better prospective husband because he has romanced me in His church. Thanks to my time living at the Jesus Burgers house and being a part of IVC, I've experienced the authentic presence of God, first through my body and then through my head.

ALWAYS MEANT FOR JESUS

JUSTIN HUNTSMAN

66 Life is a kick in the shorts," as my Uncle Don used to say. He had a good point. The gift of existing 86,400 seconds a day is such a thrill. All these seconds accumulated over the years have brought me to a place of thankfulness. And it's all due to finding the supreme meaning of life and happiness. It didn't take a PhD either. Where I am today and who I have become is nothing short of miraculous. The mighty transformation that occurred in my life after the span of a short twenty-two years can only be attributed to Jesus Christ and the glory and grandeur of God. This small story is just a glimpse of the many grand ideas of God, a small section in the whole scheme of His plan. It's almost hard to communicate in a few pages of a testimony a whole life of experiences and adventures. But the bottom line is this: it's all about Jesus. And I knew I was always meant for Him.

From childhood, it was evident that I, a rambunctious boy with a great imagination and a high tolerance for fun, had a wild adventure ahead of me. And Jesus knew this most of all. He was right there enjoying watching my silly little boyhood unfold into a similarly silly adulthood. And when I finally came around, He rejoiced at my responding to His voice in absolute surrender, all the while foreordaining my inevitable move to a groovy beach and college town known as Isla Vista many years later. Jesus gave me many opportunities for fun growing up. And though I forgot that for a couple of years, I learned in the end that He is the epitome of FUN. You heard me: F.U.N. Happiness and fun have always been, and continue to be, core values in my life. If you think I have had a whole heck of a lot of fun in my life, and have truly kissed happiness itself on the lips, you couldn't be more right. Having a good time is what I've always been about, though my idea of a good time has definitely changed over the years.

The apple didn't fall far from the tree either. My pops holds the award for the most fun Homo sapiens ever created. I'm serious. The guy was a happy guru who loved Jesus Christ and always wanted to have a good time. Mom was a kind, caring soul to accompany pops, whose tender love has always reminded me most of Divine love. That leaves my three angel sisters, who could attest to my interesting personality and unparalleled silliness in pretty much all situations. All this is to say my family actually felt like a family. We were more than just functional; there was love, and it came from Jesus

We grew up in the church. We knew the Bible verses. I learned a lot about Jesus. The only problem was I never really knew Him as a person. There was legalism in my home that tinged all the love and knowledge. There wasn't much room for failure either. There were rules in our religion, and I couldn't keep up.

I loved Jesus, I loved His words, and I loved doing the right thing. But despite this genuine love, I didn't always make the wisest choices and decisions. I was influenced by the world and bought into the lies it told me. And when I was fourteen, loving Jesus and following all the rules wasn't really fun any more, and it definitely wasn't cool.

Above everything else, I wanted to be cool as a kid. I wanted to be different; I wanted to be noticed. My image and maintaining those standards of cool was the most important thing for a long time. When I was fourteen, how my family viewed me faded in importance as my friends' perspective of me became paramount.

The adventures of a little boy eventually turned into adolescent mischief, which then turned into big trouble, which eventually led to great pain and regret. It all happened really fast. Did I learn a lot in my teenage years? The answer is a resounding yes, but at a great cost.

I was addicted to heroin and oxycodone (an opiate similar to morphine) at age seventeen. Just like that I was enslaved to narcotics, and it was an evil period of my life. Drugs became my identity. My life was reduced to spending all of my hard-earned money on pills and sacks, and watching my friends waste away. Worst of all, I didn't even care about my family and Christ because all of my being was compromised. All of who I used to be was consumed by the need for drugs.

I witnessed some sad things in those years: there was incarceration for friends, hurt for my family, and depression and despair for me. My friends and I went from average kids who wanted to have fun to drug addicts who were strung out all day. We became powerless slaves to our addictions. I don't wish for anyone to have to learn the hard way like I did.

When things get hard, people generally turn to

what they know is true. The love of God wasn't true for me yet, but I knew the true feeling heroin would give me. The euphoria and numbness that helped me feel something was all too true. I was trapped. I couldn't get out, no matter how much I wanted to leave my addiction. I lost touch with the most important things in life.

I always knew God was there, and I knew I wanted to be right with Him. But, I also knew that meant I had to be all in. It was everything or nothing.

I made the decision at the ripe age of eighteen to give my life back to Christ Jesus after a short number of years of being distant from Him. I remember exactly where I was when I heard Him audibly say, "This is not the life I have for you. I have placed a calling on your life, and it's time to get serious about getting right with Me. I love you, and you're still my son!" That was all I needed. How could I not respond to that? God had spoken! No rehab could fix me at that point. I knew what I needed to do was to be right with the Lord.

I had a lot of work to do to become close again with God: first, I got rid of my cell phone; second, I moved away; third, I asked Jesus for His help to be clean and stay clean. I went camping alone in the woods of Big Sur, California, for three hard months and kicked opiates by the grace of Jesus. Hallelujah forevermore! Liberation for the oppressed! I knew I was always meant for Jesus.

One thing led to another, and before I knew it I was enrolled in Calvary Chapel Bible College, the first of several very specific places God sent me in order to shape me into the man I am today. I stayed clean there, finally understood what it was to have a relationship with God, got a foundation in the Bible, and met two of my three best friends there. I cannot thank God enough for these two men who made me who I am today: Mac Montgomery, who showed me that loving Jesus was fun and exciting, and Erik Mason, who showed me you can be a cool surf bum while also a gnarly man of God. These guys took me to new levels.

I got rocked by the love of Jesus, too. More and more, Christ freed me from the attachment to drugs, and freed me from the idea that I had to do the right thing to earn His approval and love. I was truly a new man as the love of God showed me what I was always missing and had always been looking for: His love.

After a year at Bible College, I moved to the beach in San Diego to live at a Calvary Chapel church building and to intern with Erik. I learned discipline there, and was experiencing, for the first time, community in the family of God. It was an amazing experience interning at the church, and God had new and wonderful things to come. I can remember being in San Diego one fall day when Mac, my friend from Santa Barbara, called me.

He said, "Hey man! So, since your one-year internship is ending at the church, you should move up here to Santa Barbara! God is doing crazy things here, and I know you gotta be up here!" So I moved.

I knew in my heart it was right to be in IV, just like I knew I had to move away from my hometown to get clean from drugs. God knew this move was strategic. A strictly college town, Isla Vista is a hotbed for community, family, another Jesus movement, and radical ministry. Mac and I lived in the ministry house, known by the city as the Jesus Burgers house. In this house in the middle of the madness, we were there to do ministry on the weekends and to feed drunk kids hamburgers from our grill in the front yard. This happened every weekend. Come to our house to get a burger, get loved on by really caring Jesus people, and leave being touched by God's love. Now that's what I call a party. It's a little different from the other parties, but it's a party nonetheless.

What makes Jesus Burgers so wonderful is that Jesus is there! The spirit of Jesus lives at our house. It sounds crazy, but it's true. That is one of the main reasons people feel so good at our home. They were made to feel that way. To feel loved, cared for, valued, and embraced. That is exactly how I felt coming into the family of believers at Isla Vista Church and Jesus Burgers. Here, real Christians celebrate new life in a place known for sin. Yeah, that sounds about right. Sounds like what Jesus did, bringing liberation to a place where there were so many hurting, oppressed people.

God was not done with me either. There is always more for a child of God. Always. I began to know God as my loving Father rather than a harsh rule maker. As I moved into a state of intimacy and further into the church, I began to find freedom from trying to earn God's favor. I learned that God likes to have fun, too. I learned that the church is not an institution and not a building; church is the body of Christ—and what a good body it is, too.

These people carry the Kingdom in them, and these people know God. One of the most valuable things I learned from them was that I can hear God. It was an absolutely incredible revelation that God wanted to speak to me, whether through the Bible, through conversation, or through numerous other things. That shifted something in me. All of it came from the truth that Jesus is the only and final way to approach God and to know Him in relationship. I always knew I was meant for Jesus.

The prompting of the Holy Spirit got me to be a regular in the IV streets during those glorious weekends. I am an advocate of prayer, and God gave me the bold ability to ask people if I could pray for them. We would have huge prayer circles in the streets with ten or so people, or small prayer circles in the grass in our front yard with freshman guys with weed in their pockets. Either way, people were undeniably touched.

I can remember one night in particular when a girl with her boyfriend and her friend walked by me to leave our yard and announced, "Let's go drink."

I locked eyes with her for a few seconds and responded confidently, "You know you don't really want to drink."

"But I'm bored," she reluctantly stated back, as if that was a valid excuse.

Something inside me came alive, and I said, "Do you want to encounter Jesus right now, so you won't have to be bored another day in your life?"

The girl responded with a yes faster than I could have anticipated. I immediately commanded her boyfriend to put his hand on her so we could pray for her. By the middle of my prayer, as I was asking Jesus to meet her, she quietly but honesty interrupted me midsentence with the words, "I can feel Him."

Simple.

The last thing she said before they vanished into the night were these amazing words, "I don't want to drink anymore."

The thing is, God gives you something better than what you thought brought you happiness or some sense of satisfaction. It's really a ridiculous exchange: His love for your loneliness, fear, and depression; His amazingly satisfying presence for drugs and alcohol. It's a no brainer to me. People just need to hear that. They need to hear that they have a Father in Heaven who is really there and who cares.

In the end, we all want to know who we are and that we are loved. Jesus tells us just that. He gives us value, purpose, and reason to breathe our next breath. Life isn't a mindless existence; it is much, much more.

My life is a testimony of a beautiful mess that has been fully redeemed by Jesus and His great love. It's been almost four years since I got clean from heroin, and I couldn't be more grateful that I am found in Him. Jesus knew I was looking for fun. It took a little while, but I found out that He was fun. I wandered into the best party of all and decided to stay there for eternity.

There is a little place in the middle of the California coast where the God of the Cosmos is at a grill in a front yard meeting broken college kids on Friday nights. He's meeting them where they are and blowing their minds with His mercy and grace. Kids are coming out of gnarly bondage, just like I did. It's not always pretty, but it's far too glorious to miss.

4

THE WORKING OF MIRACLES

PROPHESYING AND HEALING IN ISLA VISTA

"FOR THE KINGDOM OF GOD DOES NOT
CONSIST IN WORDS BUT IN POWER."

—I CORINTHIANS 4:20 (NASB)

THE LOVE
AND POWER
OF GOD

SCOTT MARTINIS

I had a unique upbringing: my dad has a PhD in physics and today is working to build a quantum computer at the University of California, Santa Barbara; and my mom has a masters in molecular biology. Both are Christians. From a young age, I grew up watching Nova (a PBS science program) and other educational programs. The unspoken questions in our family when trying to decide an issue were these: What is the truth? What is the science? What are the facts?

My mom became a Christian because she had difficulty replicating reactions in her graduate laboratory that have to happen billions of times a day in order for life to exist. My dad, as he puts it, "read the Bible and thought it was true" while he was doing his post-doctorate physics research in France. I decided to follow Jesus for similar reasons.

When I was eight, I went to a conference with my dad. Speakers presented the scientific evidence that points to God. I remember being struck by something Dr. Hugh Ross said that night, "It would be more likely for enough cold air molecules to randomly come together and freeze someone solid than it would be for the universe to have spontaneously come together without a designer."

That night I was sold. I knew about Jesus and His relationship with God, and if there was a God, then I was going to formally give my life to Him. I signed a sheet of paper saying I belonged to Jesus.

In eighth grade I decided I wanted to become a Navy SEAL and go to the Naval Academy. I made it to the Naval Academy, but after two years, I decided to leave to do a missions trip. I started working with Jeff Shaffer, a former pastor who cares for Santa Barbara's poor and homeless. After a short time, I decided I would rather do something for God than return to the Naval Academy. When I mentioned to him that I was interested in attending UC Santa Barbara, Jeff suggested I visit Isla Vista Church. I attended IVC on and off for about ten months before I went to Jesus Burgers consistently. God had to train me first before He could use me there.

My introduction to miracles came in fall 2010, when Chad Dedmon came to Santa Barbara and talked about some of the miracles he had seen. That night during a ministry time, I saw someone's leg supernaturally grow and another man's back get healed. Later I prayed for someone, and God healed him. I immediately started praying for people and saw partial healings.

Not long after that I read a book on Christian mysticism, which led me to a radical decision: I decided to live every moment of every day obeying the will of God. I would ask Him what to eat, what to wear, where to go, and what to say to everyone I met. I made a lot of mistakes, but I developed a conversational relationship with God through that process, which changed my life enormously.

In 2011, God started sending me all over Santa Barbara to prophesy and pray for healing for the sick and injured. I witnessed hundreds of healings during this time. Supernatural healing became a normal part of my life. After one week when I saw forty healings (thirteen in one day), God told me to stop counting healings and to focus on loving people.

At this point, I had become a little crazy; without spiritual covering or accountability, I was running around praying and prophesying over everything in sight. God addressed this undisciplined behavior, and in the course of a few days, three or four people rebuked me. It was a hard time for me, but through God, I grew enormously. Within a few months, Jason Lomelino, pastor of Isla Vista Church, invited me to be his intern.

I was finally ready to go to Jesus Burgers on a consistent basis. God had trained me, and it was time to start loving IV. I love seeing the supernatural, so as soon as I got to Jesus Burgers, I took a "Free Prayer" sign and a "Spiritual Readings and Healing" sign onto the streets. I wasn't comfortable prophesying yet, but that changed very quickly. If someone comes up to a spiritual readings sign, they usually come with an expectation that you will say something prophetic to them. That realization helped me enormously. Their expectation helped draw prophecy out of me.

The school year drew to a close, and Jesus Burgers was shutting down for the summer. God told me to take a spiritual readings sign out to Del Playa Drive every Friday night. Amazing things began to happen that summer as God and I poured out His love to Isla Vista.

One night a few girls came up to the spiritual readings sign, and I began to prophesy over them. They were all amazed at what God had shown me about them—so touched that they brought their friends over. Their friends experienced God as well, and soon they brought more people to me. That night over ten people just from that group came to receive prophecy.

One of my favorite experiences was when a girl walked by and I felt led to offer her prayer. She called me a "Christ fag" and initially rejected my offer. I kept talking with her and discovered someone had stolen thousands of dollars worth of camera equipment from her. Photography was her passion and now she felt frustrated and unloved. She didn't think anyone was really committed to her, or that anyone cared enough to pursue her, no matter what. My goal that night was to prove her wrong. I shared that God loves us no matter what, that He never gives up on us, and that He doesn't ask anything in return when He pours out His love. I talked with her for more than an hour and ended up praying with her.

I am convinced that God's love is most purely expressed when we give it without asking for anything in return. We don't have to first shape up or do the right things in order to experience His love—He will love us where we are.

One night I saw a student with a cast on his arm walking down Del Playa. I knew God wanted to heal him, since God is a healer. I found out that this student had broken his collarbone, so I told him God wanted to heal him and asked if I could pray for him.

"I'm drunk; isn't God mad at me?" he said. After I reassured him that God loved him no matter what, he let me pray for his collarbone. Almost instantly, his arm stopped hurting, and he could even raise it over his head (which should be impossible with a broken collarbone). He was surprised, to say the least, and he told me that if it still did not hurt in the morning, he would go to church. I never saw him again, but I trust that man was changed.

One night a man I had prayed for previously came to our "Spiritual Readings and Healing" sign with back pain. He believed that my prayers could heal him, but he wanted to see if someone else's prayer could heal him. A girl in our ministry, Heather, prayed for him in Jesus' name. God healed him that time, too. She asked if he wanted to receive Jesus. He did!

Afterward the student said, "I want to follow Jesus, but I really like smoking pot." We responded, "Jesus is better than pot! Let us prove it to you." We prayed that he would experience the Holy Spirit, and he immediately felt the joy of God's presence. "Dude, I feel extra high!" he exclaimed. Jesus truly came to give us abundant life.

On another night, two men came up wanting to experience God. I have a lot of faith that God wants people to experience Him, so I told them we would pray and God would speak to them and show Himself. One man felt the love of God, and in his mind's eye saw an image of bright light. The other guy, a Jewish man, saw a vision of God the Father seated on His throne in Heaven with a golden scepter in His right hand. He did not see Jesus anywhere. I invited the man to pray again and ask for a revelation of Jesus. Shortly afterward he saw a vision of Jesus sitting, as he put it, "in a little cubbyhole-kind-of-thing at the side of the throne." He saw Jesus sitting on the Mercy Seat (a relatively obscure image in the Bible, which I doubt this man knew about before), and the man was trying to find words to describe what he saw in his vision.

Miracles are amazing: I love it when someone sees that God is real through the supernatural. Ultimately though, Jesus Burgers is really about changing a city.

This ministry brings together our American college culture and a party, and redeems both into an encounter in which people can experience the love and presence of God. Jesus Burgers is about creating a better party; it's about redeeming the culture of our city—and in the process, transforming our city. God doesn't want the parties to stop in Isla Vista; He wants to improve them by filling them with His love. When the Holy Spirit fills Isla Vista, the parties will not stop; they will only get much, much, much better. Not only that, the city will be radically different because of God's tangible presence.

BECOMING A SON, HEARING HIS VOICE

CALEB MASON

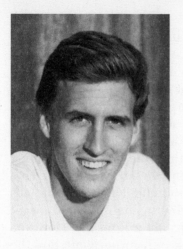

You say you have a relationship with God. Might I ask you to consider what this relationship looks like? Does it consist of dry, unanswered, unending prayers that feel like you are talking to a wall most of the time? For many of us, this has been the majority of our spirituality as we have experienced it, and this was the unsatisfying reality I lived in for many years.

The second oldest of five, I was born into a very evangelistic family that strived to uphold moral living. As far as I understood, loving God was about obeying His commandments, and that was how I would gain His approval. When I failed to uphold those standards, however, the guilt and condemnation would come rushing into my mind and my heart like a flood. This caused me to create a great distance between God and me. No matter how hard I tried, I would fail yet again. Living for God seemed so impossible to me that eventually I just gave up. Then, divorce shattered our family.

My parents were my spiritual role models, and when their marriage failed, it proved to me that living for God really was impossible. My world contradicted itself.

I spiraled down into the temptations that the world continually threw at me, and by the time I was only eleven years old, I was consistently smoking pot and drinking alcohol. These things seemed to numb the pain, and I felt like I was at least having fun. Anything seemed better than the pain in my family and the broken relationships I was dealing with. This lasted through high school, and I had become addicted to sex, partying, drinking, fighting, and drugs. I was ruining relationships all around me. However, God supernaturally started transforming me, and the true change was in my heart.

My best friend told me he felt like he was in love with God, similar to the way it felt to be in love with a girl. I couldn't believe what I was hearing. I knew that if he could feel that way, I could too. But my lifestyle didn't change much at that point.

Then one night at a party, I walked into a bathroom, looked in the mirror, and saw myself standing there utterly lifeless and dead. Out of my mouth, God spoke these words to me, "Why are you doing this to yourself? You know that I LOVE you, son." I ran out of that bathroom in complete shock.

Over the next three months, my desires started drastically changing. God was pursuing me in every way. I couldn't get my mind off of Him. The more I thought about and meditated on Him, the more I wanted Him. I was becoming addicted to God! I eventually completely surrendered control of my life to Him, and wanted nothing more than to fall more in love with the person of Jesus. I was experiencing the love of God in such a real way that my life had been transformed, even though none of my circumstances had changed.

I began to pray and read my Bible consistently and to attend a church with young people who were also pursuing God in radical ways. I had a genuine relationship with God. I visited Isla Vista Church on the weekends and ventured out to participate in this thing called Jesus Burgers that I had been told about. In IV, I saw thousands of young people wandering the streets, partying, drinking, smoking, fighting, and hooking up with each other. I was taken aback because what I was looking at were people just like me. God had just snatched me out of that lifestyle. There I stood watching people doing what I had been doing, but this time I saw them with brand new eyes!

I fell in love with the city of Isla Vista and eventually moved into the Jesus Burgers house solely to be a missionary to the city. I was blessed to live with some of the most amazing men and women. We were having a blast serving the King of Kings together. Even so, sometimes I wondered: Does God really hear my prayers? Is He really there? I mean, I spend a whole lot of time talking to Him, but I still don't hear Him talking to me. Is this a one-sided relationship? But God knew my thoughts and feelings, and He had a plan to change them.

One night at Jesus Burgers, the daughter of a well-known prophetic minister asked me if I knew how to prophesy. I thought: Prophesy? Like Moses and Elijah? I had no idea what she was talking about. So I answered with a simple no and told her I didn't really understand what prophecy was. She laughed with excitement and her eyes lit up. She said, "Ok, so when we walk up to the next person, ask God in your head if He has anything He wants you to say to that person. Then, the first thing that comes to your mind, say it! Who cares if it's wrong!" I was terrified, to say the least. She grabbed me by the arm and said, "Let's go!" I couldn't believe she was actually going to make me do this.

We walked up to a guy and girl standing in the line to get a hamburger, and my friend started talking to them. As I stood there, everything I thought I knew about having a relationship with God was in question. In my head, I started praying. My prayer went something like, "Hi there, God. Um, I'm not exactly sure what I am asking for. But, if there's anything you want to say, here I am." A few seconds later as I stood there with my head down, feeling extremely awkward and uncomfortable, this thought entered my mind: He is a protector of women. That was the entire thought. I laughed at myself. Yeah, right. Good one, you sneaky imagination, you. A few minutes later, after she was done talking with them, she looked at me and said with a smile, "Get anything?" I was stuck! I had no place to run! This was going to be embarrassing. I reluctantly said, "Well, I don't know. I guess . . . (stumbling for words) He is a protector of women." Instantly the girl standing next to her boyfriend shouted, "Oh my God! How did you know that? He totally is!" I stood there, literally with my jaw dropped. "Did God really just tell me that? He did! No way. I can't believe this, that really just happened!" Those were the things going through my mind at that moment. We proceeded to talk to the couple and share the love of God with them. The girl went further and explained exactly how her boyfriend had always protected the women in his life.

As the night went on, I felt like I was as high as a kite. I prophesied over eight more people, getting prophetic words of knowledge about their families, situations, and relationships. I also received words of wisdom for people in their unique situations. These individuals were having supernatural experiences, and it radically opened up their hearts to hear the good news about Jesus. I laughed and cried with them, and I was able to see two people receive Jesus that night as their Lord, Master, Savior, and Lover. My life as I knew it surely was at a major turning point.

I woke up the next day and jumped out of bed, as I couldn't wait to talk to God again. I began listening to God when I was alone. I started cultivating a lifestyle of hearing the voice of God and sharing what I heard with people. There were a handful of us in the house and in the church who were experiencing these things together, and some who had already been walking in them. Prayer began to take on an entirely new meaning to me. Instead of rambling on and on with impressive Biblical and spiritual prayers, I started shutting my mouth and quieting my mind. I did this so that I could simply listen. As I listened, I began to hear the truths and promises God was communicating to me as His son. I was becoming a sheep that knew his Shepherd's voice.

I couldn't believe that after all of these years I had spent in the church, with pastors and on mission trips, I had never once heard about this. It felt like the easiest thing I had ever done. It also felt like the most powerful thing I had ever done. It took the pressure and responsibility of coming up with clever words off of me, and I began trusting the things God was saying. Sure I got it wrong sometimes, but I believe when prophecy is presented humbly, it's perfectly okay to be wrong and move on. The goal is love, and love never fails.

Doing ministry in the streets of Isla Vista is such a blessing. One of the single most valuable things I have learned is to always remember that each individual walking the street has their own story. They have their own families, pains, fears, gifts, and qualities, as they too were made in the image of God. When I tap into the heart of God, and see what He sees, it becomes much easier to see the gold in each one. Once I see the gold in them, I can start to pull it out and encourage them. Through listening to His voice, I can share His heart for them. I am inviting people into the identity I've gained, knowing I am a son who is loved and embraced by his Father.

No Longer Called Cursed, But Children of God

Erik Mason

At the time of writing this, I have been part of Jesus Burgers for one year, and I had been visiting the Jesus Burgers house for a few years before that. I am a lead pastor for the Upper Room (which takes place before Jesus Burgers through Isla Vista Church). I feel a mighty calling and destiny. The Holy Spirit is alive, well, and active in my life and flowing out of me to see people be healed and restored. That sounds pretty great if you ask me. It's hard to think that only a short time ago, I thought God hated me, I was cursed, and the Holy Spirit could not dwell in me. Not so great anymore, huh?

So, how does one get from miserable existence to ecstatic joy and empowerment? And what all does this have to do with Jesus Burgers?

My story starts in the United States' most northern state, Alaska, where I was born and raised. Growing up, I had a wonderful life full of opportunity. My parents were married (and still are), we were never without sufficient income, and I always had a group of close friends. All this to say, I had no reason to feel any sort of discontentment. My mother began to believe in Jesus when I was five, and my whole family started to go to church. All in all, I had a pretty amazing life etched out for me.

But my youth was not some happy fairytale; at an early age, waves of darkness and depression swept in. I don't really know how or why depression became such a resounding part of my life, but most of my memories are engraved in my mind with a hazy, grey, lifeless shading. I have never been abused, had a traumatic experience, or suffered any incident that would initiate a dark time for me. Yet, depression and negativity played a cyclical theme in my life from a young age to my early adult years—despite having been an involved and active Christian.

All my life I had desired one thing from God and that was to hear His voice. No matter how good (as I considered good) I was, or how much I studied the Bible or preached the Gospel, I still felt very distant from God; eventually, I presumed I was cursed because I had committed many sins while being aware of God's salvation. I was addicted to sensual/sexual experiences while I was a youth leader, a worship leader, a teacher, and a missionary. I often struggled with the verses from the Bible that seemed to condemn me, yet I was oblivious to verses that would have affirmed and encouraged me. I believe that all these things, such as the depression, self-abasement, and distancing from God, were based on an experience that I had had earlier in life that left me to conclude that God didn't want to speak to me, and He wouldn't, no matter what I did.

It wasn't until I was twenty that I had a radical prophetic experience with God that shattered the lie that I was cursed and God hated me. It changed everything. I could write numerous pages trying to recount this experience and the immense significance it has played in my life. For now, the best analogy is that it is like seeing a distant mountain that you will one day try to summit, yet you fail to achieve the goal—never being able to break through the clouds and make the final ascent. When all hope is lost and you finally come to terms with your perpetual slipping, someone takes you by the hand and leads you through the clouds to the glorious sun break of the mountain's peak. Nothing can be compared to that incomprehensible sense of joy.

Soon after my radical experience, I was visiting the Bible College in Murrieta, California, where I had graduated the previous year. During that visit I met two gentlemen: Mac Montgomery and Justin Huntsman. I'd love to reminisce on the wild times we had after that point, but the necessary detail is that Mac moved back to Santa Barbara and started being involved with Isla Vista Church. This bridged a gap to a place that I had heard of briefly in Bible College as one of chaotic and anarchical partying. People talked about Isla Vista in the way they talk about the horrors of a war zone or an adulterous affair: apprehensively and uneasily.

Eventually, Justin had made a few visits, and I finally made my first visit on Halloween of 2009—and what a night it was. A few friends and I had driven up from Oceanside to participate in the Friday outreach called Jesus Burgers. I remember battling with fear in the Upper Room. I had not seen such a thing as Halloween weekend in Isla Vista. I grew up in a quiet, isolated area of Alaska where there are only one and a half people per square mile; we joke that there are probably more bears than people. Isla Vista, specifically Del Playa, had more people on the streets that Halloween weekend than are in most of the cities near my hometown. It was loud, crowded, and scandalous.

That night, I felt like there was an oppressive spirit waging war on my peace; I was almost shaking, and not from the cold Halloween night. Several of us (I can't quite recall the actual number, but the room was packed) gathered into the prayer shed behind the Del Playa house to worship. The peace of God was stronger and louder than the outside commotion. We couldn't hear the dubstep, yelling and screaming, and sirens of the streets; we just heard each other singing our hearts out and worshiping as if we were truly in Heaven. This was the first spiritual reality that God taught me from Jesus Burgers: that the littlest bit of light is always stronger and brighter than the darkest darkness. We weren't scared or tempted or beat down anymore. We went out onto the streets, into the massive collection of bodies wandering up and down Del Playa, and we sowed all that we had into the lives and hearts of the kids there that night. We were up until three or four in the morning, and it seemed I experienced every emotion a human can experience. We had fun and laughed with people, making *Star Wars* jokes with the kids dressed up as storm troopers, and we cried and prayed with people who had experienced real hurt. I realized that there was something completely unique happening at these Jesus Burgers outreaches.

When we returned to Oceanside after the weekend, I tried to explain to my friends what I had experienced, but it was so good and so different that I found it difficult to describe. It felt real, organic, and alive. I started telling people that "Jesus Burgers and Isla Vista Church is where the supernatural becomes natural" and that it was "the place where prophecy is as common as conversation." I started visiting more often. The people helping out at Jesus Burgers were the most powerful and loving people I had ever met, and easily some of the most authentic worshipers.

There is a real difference between all the other outreaches I have done and those by Jesus Burgers. When you get together a group of people who believe that the power of the Holy Spirit is for today and that God wants to prophesy through us, heal through us, and change lives through us, things happen. It's a family that genuinely loves God, each other, and all people. It's a family that believes what the Bible says straightforward, the promises and truth of God, Heaven and Earth, the Kingdom, and each of our own personal identities in Christ. I personally have experienced physical and spiritual healing and manifestations at Jesus Burgers, but what really astonished me and completely reformed my old perspective of spirituality was what I saw through others and my own hands: physical and spiritual manifestations, miracles, taking place with "sinners"—with unsaved people!

At Jesus Burgers, a lifelong desire has become a reality: I hear His voice. I have experienced instances of talking with unsaved people and having words of knowledge about them or pictures and visions about their lives. One time while talking with two sisters, I saw a "picture" of tents in the woods and also a "word" of the fact that they grew up camping with their father, and how that fact had something to do with their relationship with God. We had not talked at all about those details of their lives, and the sisters were fairly shocked that I knew. I told them a lot of truth about their lives and how God truly loves them, and that I knew all of this because God speaks. The story of these sisters and my visions for them is not unique. This happens all the time at Jesus Burgers. We have prayed for people to get healed and sober, and I've seen it happen. Some of the most glorious stories aren't even miraculous.

On one occasion, a group of friends all told me they hated God because their friend died in a car wreck the year before. I didn't have to prophesy or pray for healing or do something outrageous, all I had to do was listen as they cried and poured out their hearts—that was powerful enough. Eventually, they were so open with me that I got to tell them the truth: their friend was not hated by God, and God was more heartbroken than they were. Some nights aren't so dramatic and are just honest to goodness fun! There was a night when it rained all night, so three of us literally danced all over the street. That was really fitting at the time.

Jesus Burgers is not an outreach that attempts different techniques to convince people of the gospel. It is a celebration of Christ's love for us and for the world as we intercede for the city of Isla Vista in prayer and power. There's no guile or gimmick. Jesus Burgers is about the times when we're on Del Playa and it's completely freezing and the wind is slicing through our three-layer sandwich of jackets and flannels and the frost is making the ground sparkle, yet there are literally thousands of girls in the most fashionable, next-to-nothing outfits who need our jackets; we give them ours even though we'll never see them again. It's about telling a girl that she is worth so much more to God than the hell that she is putting herself through. It's about flipping over a blacked-out drunk guy so he doesn't choke on his own vomit, and then wrapping him in blankets so he doesn't get seriously sick. An action that simple will do infinitely more than the church's historical response of, "Repent, you dirty rotten worthless sinner," and the less radical, "Um . . . excuse me . . . excuse me, would you like to hear the gospel? . . . You can say no. . . . " Love is much more powerful. Can you imagine never feeling loved your whole life, then while you're partying and feeling like God hates you, someone walks up and says, "Hey, would you like a free burger?" Then that person talks to you, listens to you, and prays for you. People have admitted to us at Jesus Burgers that we showed them the first love they ever felt from people.

I am now extremely happily married, having escaped the misery I used to feel. I have found meaning and purpose through the people at Jesus Burgers. At Jesus Burgers, people have established a real connection and a powerful relationship with God and His mighty presence. They desire to bring that to the world, so that all may know that they are no longer cursed by sin—that sin's power was broken at the cross for them. Jesus became the curse so that they may no longer be cursed. If only someone would have told me that ten years ago, I can only imagine the dramatic difference it would have made in the way I viewed God and how I thought He viewed me.

FROM
ATHEIST TO
JESUS FREAK

CARSTEN QUINLAN

In 2010 I graduated from UC Santa Barbara in the top 1 percent of my class. I completed a triple major with a bachelor of science in physics and bachelor of arts degrees in mathematics and history. I came to UCSB as a dedicated atheist and left four years later as a sold-out Jesus Freak. My testimony of becoming a Christian contains pain and sorrow, as well as tremendous victory and joy. Jesus Burgers will always hold a special place in my heart because of its part in my story.

Since childhood I have been striving to discover as much truth as possible. I came to college wanting to know how the world worked. I thought if I took enough classes in the sciences and humanities, I would achieve a high level of understanding. To some degree I was correct. Eventually, I ran head-on into a huge problem—a problem that ultimately crushed my atheistic worldview. My problem was that I actually cared about doing good in the world and fighting rampant evil. From an atheistic perspective, this desire made no sense at all.

My heart told me to fight evil any way I could. Reason told me that such a desire was not rational because it required sacrifice that could never be re-paid. I resolved to go on an intellectual and spiritual journey in an attempt to solve this problem.

Though I was an atheist, I decided that religion could be a good place to start looking for answers. From among all the historical figures I studied, Jesus seemed to have it right. The Sermon on the Mount in Matthew was the first Biblical passage that really drew my attention. During my sophomore year of college, I abandoned atheism and accepted Christianity.

When I initially accepted Christianity, I did not actually know if it was true or not. Jesus Burgers changed that! I got involved with the ministry and put my new faith to the test. Over time, I came to know that the gospel was objectively true.

I used to think that religion must be accepted on the grounds of faith alone. I was mistaken. Christians have the authoritative power to work miracles of heal-ing and other wonders through the power of God. Christianity can be put to a remarkable test of valid-ity: believers ought to be able to perform miracles in Jesus' name.

So I decided to try. In the summer of 2010, some friends and I sought miraculous power from God. Just as I had been working as an experimental physi-cist, I began to do "experimental" Christianity!

We fasted, prayed, worshiped, and endured count-less awkward and embarrassing moments of praying for people in public without seeing any healings at all. But there were miracles on the way. The first one I experienced was while praying for an epileptic stu-dent in my history class. He was having a seizure, and when I prayed for him, the seizure left immediately.

As the months went by, we heard more amazing stories from people who had gone on mission trips and had seen blindness, cancer, and deafness healed.

I was so excited about the prospects of being a radical, healing Christian that I seriously contemplated foregoing graduate school. Eventually, I decided to do both.

I was at Jesus Burgers almost every weekend during 2010. We would always begin the night with worship. We would pray and make burger patties. I would often be in charge of setting up the bonfire that we had on the patio. Of course, the burgers and the fire were not the main point. Our purpose was to love Isla Vista.

Most of us lived in Isla Vista and knew the evil things that happened there. We were not ignorant of the drunkenness, the drug use, the fornication, or other ungodly behaviors. After all, most of us had been redeemed from Isla Vista. I was a former atheist and had done my share of partying. Others in our church were former drug addicts and drug dealers. We had all types at Isla Vista Church, but God was molding each of us into the image of Jesus.

If you showed up at the house, we would love you and give you a free burger. We handed out hundreds every night. We would talk to you. We would pray for you. We would let you throw up in our bathroom or living room. We would get you a glass of water and give you warmth by the fire. My nights there have created some of the fondest and dearest memories of my life.

In August 2010, two specific nights of ministry solidified within me that God was real and that Christianity was true.

It was August 27th and 28th, 2010, a Friday and Saturday night in Isla Vista. Isla Vista Church had a visiting missionary by the name of Yves Perriard in attendance, as well as a group of students from the Bethel School of Supernatural Ministry, led by Chad Dedmon.

Yves had the idea to make some large signs that said "Free Prayer" and "Free Healing." I was given the task and went over to Home Depot to buy spray paint and plywood. That evening we took the signs out onto Del Playa and began to offer prayer.

Over those two nights, I personally witnessed about a dozen healing miracles performed by myself and other members of my church. It was the most exciting two nights of my life! Here are a couple of the specific miracles I witnessed, which I wrote down immediately after they happened:

I saw this guy sitting on the curb with a cast on his right arm, so I went up to pray for him. I told him about how Jesus has given Christians authority over sickness. I prayed for him. At first, I did not feel anything, then suddenly he jerked back and said "WOW!" I was very surprised, so I asked him what he had felt. He was bewildered, looked at his cast, and exclaimed, "I got to get this thing off me!" Then he left. I was absolutely bursting with joy and confidence and love!

Next, I found a guy who had pain in his right elbow. Kyle Heiner and I prayed for him. Initially, he said, "You guys know this doesn't work, right? But whatever, go for it." I had just seen a bunch of miracles, so his doubtful statement was funny to me. Then I told him the pain was going to completely leave. Kyle and I prayed for him, and after we had said a quick prayer, I told him to test it out. When he moved his arm a bit, an absolutely bewildered look came over his face. He was totally surprised and stunned. He said, "No way, the pain is all gone!" Then Kyle and I told him that God loves him so much.

I went up to two other guys and asked if they had any pain in their body. I told them I wanted to pray for them, and that the pain would vanish. It turned out these guys were US veterans back from the war in Afghanistan. I welcomed them home and thanked them for their service to our country. Love is central to seeing miracles, so I just wanted to express my love for them. One soldier had pain in both his legs. I started praying for him, and then Yves came over and we both prayed together with Yves leading. After our prayer, we asked him to test out his knees. He began squatting down. He said he could not have done that before without pain. He was healed!

The next guy healed was named Charles. He and his friend Zack were Christians from Lompoc, California. I asked them if they had any pain, and Charles told me that his right shoulder had been hurting for most of his life. He said he had a calcium deposit. I was still quite brimming with faith and confidence, and so I prayed for him, and again, all the pain left! I asked him to test it out. I got a can of beans for him to try throwing around. He said his shoulder was now pain-free. Before the healing, throwing something like that would have hurt. So Charles got healed too!

I still keep in touch with my friends at Isla Vista Church, and I know they continue to see miracles. And they also continue to offer mercy, compassion, and friendship at the weekly Jesus Burgers barbecue. For those who desire it, they offer prayer and a chance to be led into eternal life with Christ Jesus. For those who just want a burger, they give freely, motivated by the love of God.

I am honored to have personally witnessed the reality of God's power and grace poured out upon people who were not even seeking God. I will never forget that weekend at Jesus Burgers when my life was forever changed.

POSSESSED
BY LOVE

DAVID SPURLING

I came to experience the anointing of God stirring in my life about four years ago. I had become desperately hungry. Even though none of the religious patterns made any sense to me, I set out to find God there. That was the only place I knew to look. And He was so faithful; when you seek Him, you find Him. Better still, He finds you. I read in my Bible that Jesus and His disciples did miracles, and the Apostle Paul wrote about spiritual gifts and heavenly experiences. Peter had a trance on a roof, and John saw visions of the heavenly courts and the throne of God. A guy named Phillip was transported from one part of the country to another, and people talked with angels all the time. Then I looked at my church. I looked at the Christians in my community, and I looked at my own life. There were obvious discrepancies. The more I read the Bible, the more I was convinced that the supernatural was meant to be a natural way of life when you know Jesus. I asked God, "Where on earth is the Church acting like it should be?"

That's when God showed me Bethel. In this church in Redding, California, I found all sorts of radical believers. And they were living out lives that looked really similar to the supernatural adventures lived out by New Testament believers. They did miracles, they heard from God, they prophesied, they talked with angels, they had experiences in Heaven, they prayed and changed weather, they had favor with heads of state and leaders of nations, and most of all, they really, really, really loved Jesus. In fact, more than anything else, it ended up being the love that they carried that impressed me so deeply. So I became one of them. I moved to Redding and started a three-year journey of studying the Kingdom of God, getting to know the King more and more intimately. I traveled the world, growing in my experience of the Holy Spirit and the Father heart of God. I lived big on the promises of God, and I risked hard with the very substance of my heart. A journey that is not always pain free. Building a history with God has its costs, as anyone with wisdom should attend to. But once I was possessed by love, all wisdom could see was the glory of Jesus, and all cost became negligible.

During my second year at Bethel, I met a group of people from Isla Vista. Jason and more than twenty others had made a pilgrimage to Redding to experience what God was doing. Some of them ended up sleeping on my living room floor, guys like Mac Montgomery, Justin Huntsman, Caleb Mason, and Erik Mason. They loved God and loved family, and they invited me to stay with them in Isla Vista if I ever came down that way. When I graduated second year, I wanted to road trip around Southern California, so I took them up on their offer.

My first trip through Santa Barbara was a pioneering venture. It was me and my motorcycle and an open road. I was instantly welcomed into the Isla Vista family, and my experience with Jesus Burgers impressed on my heart even more the depth of love that this community carries. I told Jason that I felt the Lord wanted me to set some roots down in Santa Barbara, whatever that meant. I just knew that I was supposed to be a part of this family.

From that point, Jason and I started discussing the possibility of a Bethel ministry trip coming down to partner with Jesus Burgers and pouring some fuel on the fire in the Isla Vista community. As our ideas grew over the summer months, a reality started to develop. Soon it was official: I would be leading a team of Bethel School of Supernatural Ministry (BSSM) students on a trip to Santa Barbara over Halloween weekend. We picked that weekend because it's the biggest party weekend of the year. We knew that God wanted to show up and show off, and we wanted to be there for it. Jesus Burgers is the best party in town, and there was a great expectation for glory that weekend.

My BSSM team was made up of nine radical revivalists in their second year. I had the pleasure of driving South with David, Christian, Kevin, Ingrid, Debora, and the engaged Marissa and Jeremy. Jesse and Jessica joined us in Santa Barbara after they had been on a four-day ministry trip out East.

Just South of San Jose, in a little town called Morgan Hill, we stopped at an In-N-Out Burger for lunch. As we were about to leave, I began to talk with the drive-thru worker. I told him where we were headed, and we made some other small talk. When I asked if he had any pain in his body we could pray for, he said he had pain in his back. I prayed a short prayer, commanding the pain to leave his body. As soon as I finished praying, he looked up and said, "Have you ever heard of Jesus Burgers?" I was shocked to hear this from him, since we were still four hours from Santa Barbara!

"Yeah, those are our friends! That's actually why

we're going to Santa Barbara!" I told him. "I've been there a few times," he commented, "they have good burgers." We asked him about his pain, and it had gone. It was as though once he had been healed that he instantly thought, I've met people like this before—who pray and God listens—at Jesus Burgers.

Over the weekend, we celebrated Jesus Burgers on both Friday and Saturday nights, since it was Halloween. We saw God do many amazing miracles; it was incredible! People would feel the presence of God around us and ask for prayer. People who were drunk on alcohol would supernaturally sober up, or come down off drugs. People would start to cry as they felt loved and valued for the first time in a long time—or ever. People met God and were saved, healed, and delivered.

Friday night, Kevin prayed for a drunk guy who wanted to experience the presence of God. Kevin had him hold out his hands and say, "Come, Holy Spirit." He did that, then said he felt a fireball go from his fingertips to his chest to his head. He immediately became sober and wept as he confessed everything he had ever done wrong. After this went on for half an hour, Kevin asked him if he wanted to receive Jesus, and he said yes. Kevin had him close his eyes and picture Jesus, and then instructed him to say to Him what he needed to say. With his eyes closed, in the Spirit, he saw a beam of light come down in front of him. He opened his heart and, through more tears, found new life in the presence of a loving God.

At one point on Saturday night, Marissa and Jeremy were inside the Jesus Burgers house. A big, drunk German guy came into the house. He had fallen flat on his face. His nose was completely swollen, bloodied, and bent sideways. It was noticeably broken. He had bruising under both eyes. They brought him into the kitchen and prayed for him. All the pain left instantly, and they watched the swelling go down and the bruising disappear! He could not believe it was happening. Furthermore, his nose straightened out completely! The only signs it had ever been broken were slight spots of bruising on the sides of the nose.

He was shocked, "How are you doing this!?"

Marissa responded with, "God just healed you!"

Then he said, "Can God heal my back too?"

They prayed for his back and his ligament injury, and both were healed!

"How are you doing these things?" he asked.

"Jesus lives in us," Marissa said. "Would you like Jesus to live in you as well?"

"Yes!" he responded. He received Jesus right there in the kitchen, and Jeremy prayed for him to receive the Holy Spirit. He came into the living room and started to tell all the people there that God is real, and that he was just healed. He was boldly and proudly proclaiming the gospel of the Kingdom!

What he didn't know was that he was witnessing to a room full of Christians! When Ingrid told him they were all Christians, he was very excited. Ingrid led him to encounter the Holy Spirit more, and then explained to him that he can talk to God, and God will talk back.

He asked, "Can God tell me where the best party is?"

Ingrid replied, "Yes, that's easy—it's right here, because Holy Spirit is here, and wherever He is is the best party."

He said with excitement, "That's right!"

On Friday night, there was a realm of peace that surrounded the Jesus Burgers house—like a big Holy Spirit hug. On Saturday night, that peace extended over the whole region, impacting hearts for Jesus. The impact that our team had was phenomenal, and

Isla Vista will never be the same. God has not given the fathers of this community a mandate to impact a subculture; He has given them a city to transform, and people to take from glory to greater glory.

At the end of the weekend, it was the thing that brought me to Santa Barbara that I had enjoyed the most: love. The love of the Father, poured out over loving children. The love of family, receiving and giving in this divine story, partaking of the nature of the person of Love Himself. These are a people who love well, and every miracle we saw on the streets was an expression of that love. I am looking forward to many more family feasts surrounding Jesus Burgers weekends. The light of Christ will illuminate how far His great love extends into the hearts of His lost children, and He's calling them home.

The road that the IV family walks will look different as the realms they are influencing start to transform with greater and greater momentum. There will never be an end to Jesus Burgers because it is all about love, but I feel as though we saw the beginning of the end of radical party ministry in this region. Soon people's minds will be renewed. They will no longer be drawn to fill the void in their lives with that lifestyle. Soon the culture of darkness will be replaced in full by a culture of light, and the kings and priests of Jesus in Santa Barbara will press into the greater glories that He has for us. Of the increase of His government and of His peace, there is no end.

Conclusion

We hope you have enjoyed reading these stories from the Jesus Burgers ministry in Isla Vista. As you can see, Jesus Burgers is about love. This love takes on many forms each week—a hamburger, a listening ear, a prophetic word from God, a place to go to the bathroom, a simple prayer, a physical healing, a ride home, or even a place to pass out.

Our prayer is for God's people to say yes to Him and to follow Him on adventures of faith that lead to reaching others with His love. May you, the reader, continue to discover the love of God and the ways He wants you to, in turn, love others, tangibly and personally.

Isla Vista Church is available to help in any way to those who would like to begin similar ministries in their own town. Please feel free to contact us with questions or if you would like more information about the ministry at jesusburgers.org@gmail.com

Thank you for taking time to read this book and to receive a glimpse into what God is doing today in the city of Isla Vista.

In Christ,
Jason Lomelino

Acknowledgments

Thank you, Jesus, for using the foolish things of the world like a hamburger to reach countless lives for Your fame and honor!

To all of those on college campuses who are laying down their lives to see the greatest wave of revival sweep across America, thank you for not giving up—through faith and patience we inherit the promises!

To my wife, Holly, I love you, beautiful. Your life more than any other has shown me Christ and what love looks like. Thank you for never wavering in unbelief through all the trials, hardships, and tests we have faced together. Leading a church and raising a family in a college town continues to be a journey of faith, and I could not ask for a better life partner, friend, and wife.

To my four children and Lord willing my unborn children who will read this book one day, each of you mean way more to me than anything in this world. Thank you for sharing your mom and me with lots of other people; it does not go unnoticed. You continue to teach me the freedom of simplicity, living loved and having fun in life. Your mom and I love each of you more than you will ever know (well at least until you get your own kids).

To the IV Church family, thank you for your faith and love. Seriously, I have the best family in the world! I could not ask to be a part of a more authentic and genuine group of people. You love well and teach others to do the same.

To Jacob and Kimberly Reeve, who led the church plant to IV in 2002, thank you for living the life of faith and not just talking about it. Your seed of faith, hope and love continues to produce an abundance. Our fruit is your fruit.

To Britt Merrick, thank you for the influence you have had on the city of IV and your faithfulness to Jesus and the gospel message.

To Gary Lomelino, Erik Krueger, and Dan Hodgson, you men have shown me Christ; your lives and faith are inspirational.

To Jeremy Klopfenstein and Robin Hulett, thank you for treating me as a younger brother when I first came to Christ (I needed those spiritual diapers and pacifiers).

To my sister Melissa, the fruit of my life is directly connected to your life and prayers; your reward for all you have done for our family awaits you in Heaven.

To my mom and little sister, Michelle, thank you for always loving with your whole hearts (two of the biggest hearts I know). I am eternally grateful for both of you.

To Dan and Erik, my brothers-in-law, I could not have asked God for two better men to have married my sisters. You have been examples of Christ to them, and for that I am eternally grateful.

To Jim, Marsha, and Jared, thank you for loving and supporting us as a family over the years. Holly could not be more thankful for the parents and brother God has given her. Our kids have such an amazing Papa Jim, Nana, and Uncle Jared.

To Shalhoob Meat Company, thank you for your generous donations of meat in the early years and Captain Phil & Lawry Smith, for your gifts of buns these last few years.

To Sea Hill Press, thank you for making this entire work a pleasure!

Thank you Daniel Hayrapetian for your connection to Sea Hill Press; you are one of the more honorable men I know.

Thank you Josh Morton and Tony Hui for contributing your artistic talents to this book (Proverb 22:29).

Thank you Mark Porter for being a brother, friend, and partner to this ministry—your faithful sowing has never gone overlooked or unappreciated, Heaven knows.

Lastly, thank you to all of you who have supported Jesus Burgers, the Lomelino family, and IV Church over the years. This book would not have been possible without you and your faithfulness both prayerfully and financially.

**MISSION
ISLA VISTA**
PARTNER TO SEE A
CITY TRANSFORMED

To support the work of God in Isla Vista and the
Jesus burgers ministry please consider becoming a
partner in our work.

WWW.JESUSLOVESIV.COM/PARTNER